CONSUMING JESUS

CONSUMING JESUS

Beyond Race and Class Divisions in a Consumer Church

PAUL LOUIS METZGER

WILLIAM B. EERDMANS PUBLISHING COMPANY
GRAND RAPIDS, MICHIGAN / CAMBRIDGE, U.K.

Published 2007 by
Wm. B. Eerdmans Publishing Co.
2140 Oak Industrial Drive N.E., Grand Rapids, Michigan 49505 /
P.O. Box 163, Cambridge CB3 9PU U.K.
www.eerdmans.com

Printed in the United States of America

12 11 10 09 08 07   7 6 5 4 3 2 1

Library of Congress Cataloging-in-Publication Data

Metzger, Paul Louis.
    Consuming Jesus: beyond race and class divisions
    in a consumer church / Paul Louis Metzger.
       p.   cm.
    Includes bibliographical references.
    ISBN 978-0-8028-3068-5 (pbk.: alk. paper)
    1. Food — Religious aspects — Christianity. 2. Dinners and dining —
    Religious aspects — Christianity. 3. Church. 4. Consumption (Economics) —
    Religious aspects — Christianity. 5. Materialism — Religious aspects —
    Christianity. 6. Race relations — Religious aspects — Christianity.
    7. Social classes. I. Title.

BR115.N87M48   2007
261.0973 — dc22

                      2007026264

With its publication, I would like to offer a toast
and the dedication of this book:

> To Dr. John M. Perkins, civil rights leader and community developer,
>> whose vision has inspired me;

> to Dr. Donald Brake, my academic dean,
>> whose vision has supported me;

> to the memory of Hannah Green, my niece,
>> whose life is a memorable vision of touching others;

> and to all those church leaders who are consumed by a far nobler vision
>> than what the consumer church culture has to offer.

Contents

Contents

Foreword

The most difficult commandment in the Bible is the instruction for Christians to maintain unity. The apostle Paul even tells us to agree with one another. Every time I read that passage I wonder how ignorant a person would have to be to make this statement without clarifying which side is right and on which issue. It is obvious to me that Paul hadn't forecasted the Christian Reformation when he gave his decree. He wasn't taking into account the coming Industrial Revolution or the subsequent commercial revolution either. These plot points on the timeline of Western history have cut the Christian church into more pieces than a deep-dish pizza. There are few areas in the Western evangelical church in which we are in greater disobedience than in this business of being one. And while I would have initially proposed a simpler solution than Dr. Metzger's, namely that everybody agree with me, Dr. Metzger has done a more noble thing by digging into the divides and studying the sharp ridges of our disconnect in an effort to understand where the partitions come from and how the pieces might fit back together.

In exploring these divides Dr. Metzger reveals the evolution of our racialization, our socio-economic divisions, and our political encampments. In reading *Consuming Jesus*, we see that many of our divisions were caused by our own ignorance, or perhaps by the manipulative tricks of the Evil One to keep us from projecting a living answer to Christ's prayer in John 17 that we be unified even as he and the Father and Spirit are unified.

Of particular interest to me was Dr. Metzger's understanding of the greater culture that surrounds the divided church. In looking at the issue, he backs his lens out to see the church as a whole, but then further to see the culture as it surrounds the church like a womb of sorts. As biblical scholarship is in decline, and as church leaders become more versed in television news than in New Testament Greek, we understand the church better, not by simply studying it, but by studying what it has eaten to become it. And when we begin to see the connections, we begin to understand ourselves and sit alone with a conviction that many of the issues we are taking "stands" on are not biblical issues but cultural issues that will not last into eternity.

Without leaving us hanging, Dr. Metzger proposes a viable solution. Perhaps the most enjoyable aspect of this book lies in the hope the author forecasts for the contemporary church, a solution not unlike a patchwork quilt, allowing our individuality to be stitched together alongside communities uniquely different from ours, and yet coming together to make an obvious and useful whole. In reading this book, one moves into the tall walls caused by these dramatic shifts and senses Dr. Metzger's grace for all parties. Through his objective perspective, we finally realize that we are rats in a maze, where before we simply searched for cheese. I encourage you to think objectively as you read this book and consider these issues, and then in action lock arms at our differences to display for the world one Christ manifesting himself through one church for one purpose, that the world might know that Jesus is the Son of God and that he came to save people's souls.

DONALD MILLER

Trading Stone Altars for Coffee Bars

I remember sitting in a U.S. immigration office several years ago, where my wife and I had showed up for an interview in the process of applying for her green card. We were about halfway through a long and arduous bureaucratic process that was not anywhere near as funny or sexy as Hollywood's version of *Green Card*. At one point in the discussion, the official sitting across the desk screamed at my wife for not having brought some document along (we had not been told to bring it). It was all so sudden and unexpected — and humiliating. I felt helpless. What could I do or say? If I had reacted with the emotions I felt, my wife's hope of getting her green card could be severely jeopardized. I sat there speechless and numb. But the event sensitized me to all the feelings of those other helpless hopefuls present there that day, those who also longed to get green cards or citizenship papers to this great country of ours.

I remember peering at the faces of Mexican applicants in that office with us, hearing their broken English, empathizing with them as they dealt with office clerks who seemed to treat them as if they were nothing more than numbers or annoying nuisances. Later I was able to reflect that, for all their apparent coldness and aloofness, these clerks were likely caring people who loved their kids. They may even have taken these jobs to put flesh on the American ideals expressed in Emma Lazarus's poem "The New Colossus," inscribed on the Statue of Liberty, which stands guard over Ellis Island:

> Here at our sea-washed, sunset gates shall stand
> A mighty woman with a torch, whose flame
> Is the imprisoned lightning, and her name
> Mother of Exiles. From her beacon-hand
> Glows world-wide welcome; her mild eyes command
> The air-bridged harbor that twin cities frame.
> "Keep, ancient lands, your storied pomp!" cries she
> With silent lips. "Give me your tired, your poor,
> Your huddled masses yearning to breathe free,
> The wretched refuse of your teeming shore.
> Send these, the homeless, tempest-tost to me,
> I lift my lamp beside the golden door!"[1]

Perhaps these clerks were once inspired by such ideals, but now those ideals appeared to be mere words — incapable of making their spirits soar. The bureaucratic system, the sheer volume of applicants, and those cheerless office walls seemed to have weighed down and restructured these officials. Their work was so important, yet so overwhelming.

The subject I address in this book is also important, and equally overwhelming. I have been sensitized by these and other similar encounters with structural coldness and insensitivity to the issues before us: race and class divisions in the consumer church. For we are also speaking here about those who are in and those who are out. And like the story above, this book concerns a personal journey. It is my personal struggle as an American evangelical to cope with consumer religion and its impact on race and class divisions in the American evangelical church.

The culture wars and the consumer culture that Christians have internalized and that have restructured us have made efforts to spread the love of Jesus increasingly difficult, which becomes clear to me when I speak to students on university campuses and meet with religious leaders and their followers from non-Christian faith traditions. Whether we

1. Emma Lazarus, "The New Colossus," in *Nineteenth-Century American Women Poets: An Anthology,* ed. Paula Bernat Bennett (Oxford: Blackwell Publishers Ltd., 1998), p. 287.

evangelicals mean to or not, we appear mean-spirited and interested only in a privileged few — upwardly mobile, white, Anglo-Saxon, Protestant, heterosexual males and their families (and, oh yes, perhaps those minority counterparts who make it to our economic and social level) — and in keeping others out. For instance, although I know he repented of his statements and reached out to some of those offended by his remarks, the late Rev. Jerry Falwell's claim that gays, lesbians, and secularists or materialists (among others) were to blame for 9/11 has left its mark on "the lost."[2]

I applauded Rev. Falwell for partnering with Roman Catholics and Mormons to speak out on the plight of the human unborn; I am grateful to Dr. James Dobson for helping parents cope with the difficult challenges they face today; and I commend Pastor Rick Warren for reaching many up-and-outers and down-and-outers. Yet we evangelicals have a long way to go in moving from the quest for church growth to the pursuit of church health, to borrow a concept from Warren's own purposeful claims in *The Purpose Driven Church*.[3] Therefore, we need to develop a sixth sense and purpose, one that is attuned to overcoming the race and class divide in American evangelicalism's consumer-market-driven outreach. All too often, the consumer-market-driven church movement is insensitive to how it divides people and locks out the "tired," the "poor," the "huddled masses," the "wretched refuse," the "homeless" — and all the others who appear to be different from us. The pursuit of an Emma Lazarus–like sixth sense and purpose has been part of my own journey, a personal journey that has been marked by my own failures to engage in a loving way those who are different from me. I am part of the problem. So I pray the Jesus prayer: "Lord Jesus Christ, Son of God, have mercy on me, a sinner."

2. For a discussion of Rev. Falwell's initial remarks about the September 11th attacks, see Gustav Niebuhr, "After the Attacks: Finding Fault; U.S. 'Secular' Groups Set Tone for Terror Attacks, Falwell Says," *New York Times,* Sept. 14, 2001 (late edition-final), Section A, p. 18. For further information, see "Rev. Falwell Blames for Terrorist Attacks," Sept. 14, 2001, last revised May 21, 2004, http://www.actupny.org/YELL/falwell.html (Nov. 2005).

3. Rick Warren, *The Purpose Driven Church: Growth Without Compromising Your Message & Mission* (Grand Rapids: Zondervan, 1995), p. 17.

All forms of disunity in the church can be traced, in the end, to an absence of *practical* love, an absence that hinders our outreach to the world. With this in mind, we should take to heart Jesus' prayer to the Father in John 17: "May they be one as we are one to let the world know that you have sent your Son" (my paraphrase). As you read this book, and long after you have put it down to press on with the cause, may you pray this prayer in your personal journey. It will change your life! More importantly, it will change the church, so that the world may come to know that the Father has sent the Son — not just for some, but for all.

one of the most significant prayers in the Bible and in history.

*　　*　　*

It is not simply what we say that matters, but also what we communicate. Sometimes, because we cannot recognize what we are communicating to others, we need an outsider's perspective. In December 2004, the *Willamette Week*, a left-of-center secular publication in Portland, Oregon, featured a cover story on Portland's evangelicals. Historically, the paper had been quite antagonistic toward evangelical Christianity; but it was now attempting to understand the evangelical community from the inside, especially given that community's role in President Bush's 2004 election victory and the passage of the constitutional amendment ballot measure in Oregon a month earlier banning same-sex marriage. The piece was entitled "The J Crew: Meet Portland's Evangelicals," with a subhead that read, "Portland's Christian soldiers may seem queer, but they're here. Get used to them." The article was, to many evangelicals, a surprisingly irenic and sympathetic piece.[4] More surprising than the tone was what the writer observed in a matter-of-fact way, with no ill intent, while reporting on the movement.

The cover gave a hint of what one could expect: it featured a *Simpsons*-like rendition of a smiling Jesus with outstretched hand, wearing a nametag that said, "HELLO, my name is Jesus." Inside the paper was a discussion of the ballot measure, references to gigantic strip-mall

---

4. Zach Dundas, "The J Crew: Meet Portland's Evangelicals," *Willamette Week*, December 1, 2004, p. 16.

churches and the like — "parking lots the size of the Sea of Galilee" filled with minivans and cars bearing the "W" campaign sticker. Then there was the discussion of Christian bookstores filled with niche-market Bibles and books on the relationship of Christian faith to business management, Rick Warren's *The Purpose Driven Life* with its spinoffs and sequels, Christian romance literature ("Think bodice-rippers, light on the ripping," the writer said), the *Left Behind* series with the "cottage industry of imitators and knockoffs" it has spawned, and the popular Bibleman videos and DVDs.[5] Something somewhat more subtle was what the writer observed about the use of sacred space. Evangelical churches are "more likely to boast a state-of-the-art sound system than a hand-crafted altar."[6]

Some of the evangelical characteristics noted by the writer no doubt reflect the churches' sophisticated marketing techniques in their attempt to engage popular culture. In this sense, the movement has been quite effective. One can simply observe those megachurches that look like strip malls and shopping malls, which stand in stark contrast to cruciform cathedrals. But how effective has the movement been in engaging human suffering, including race and class divisions in the church and society? Perhaps the absence of the altar or table at the front of many of these churches is also revealing, especially since it has given way to a coffee bar at the back.

I like a latte as much as the next person does. Coffee bars have their place — but they are problematic at the back of a sanctuary, especially when there is no Lord's table in front. That's because the coffee bar and the Lord's table are symbolic: both are symbols that communicate powerfully their use of "sacred" space. The coffee bar connotes pleasure and leisure (good things in their own right), whereas the Lord's table always connotes joy through suffering: the bloody grapes of wrath have become a river of life. Like coffee bars with their sweetly flavored lattes, many churches (subliminally) suggest that the church will provide those who attend with the very things the world does — everything involved in self-

---

5. Dundas, "The J Crew," pp. 17, 19, 21, 22, 23, 25, 26.
6. Dundas, "The J Crew," p. 21.

fulfillment. Christ, on the other hand, drank from a very different cup, one that was bittersweet, in order to bring meaning, purpose, and life.

The wine of the Lord's Supper was intended from its inception to break down divisions, for everyone was (and is) to drink from the common cup of Christ's victory amidst victimization. But when the Lord's altar is missing, replaced by technological wizardry, entertainment, and coffee bars, or when we disconnect the chalice or cup and loaf or wafer from the agape feast, we have lost that symbol. The early Christians often celebrated the Lord's Supper during the church family agape, or love feast, which was a real church potluck.

This is no parochial affair. Dr. Martin Luther King, Jr., saw his Ebenezer Baptist Church in Atlanta as a microcosm of the entire universe, which he took with him in his imagination into his civil rights battles in a way similar to how the Israelites carried the Ark of the Covenant into battle.[7] If we were to view the "latte church" as such a microcosm today, what would it look like, and what kinds of battles would we be waging? Perhaps we would look like the Moral Majority's "moral mandate" types: those who often appear to be waging special-interest, lifestyles-of-privilege legislative battles from leisurely positions of affluence that cost them nothing (other than money, time, and signatures). We often seem far removed from battles in the trenches, where people need to make personal sacrifices for the benefit of the greater good — especially for the benefit of the underprivileged.

When Christ returns, will he find faith, the kind of faith that engages suffering and breaks down walls of division between peoples — or not? What he certainly will find is some version of the shopping-mall church, with wonderful sound systems for the praise songs and a latte-to-go. If we think of latte as a new metaphor for the "opiate of the masses," we can see that the evangelical church often functions as an opiate of the consumer masses. An all-consuming house-cleaning is in order.

My criticism of the evangelical church is not the angry and cynical attack of an outsider; rather, it is the criticism of one who loves the evan-

---

7. Richard Lischer, *The Preacher King: Martin Luther King, Jr. and the Word that Moved America* (New York: Oxford University Press, 1995), pp. 16-17.

gelical church's historic values of piety and holistic outreach and mission, but one who longs for reform. Evangelicals were at the forefront historically in the fight to abolish slavery in Great Britain and the United States, and we have the presence, vitality, and energy to fight against forces such as consumerism that foster race and class divisions in America today. I love the evangelical movement, especially when we are consumed by Christ and not by consumer religion. But we do need a nobler, all-consuming vision of evangelical Christian faith.   Jolsteon

One evangelical Christian who is consumed by Christ and who offers a nobler vision of evangelical Christianity is Dr. John M. Perkins, an African-American evangelical civil rights leader from Mississippi. Born the son of a sharecropper, Perkins left Mississippi for California in his youth soon after his brother, a decorated war veteran, was murdered by a white Mississippi police officer because of the color of his skin. Perkins grew up thinking that Christianity was the white man's religion, that whites used it to keep black people down, and that Christianity's songs were merely an opiate for the black masses. Although Perkins had only reached the fifth grade in school, he was able to land a good job in California and raise a family under decent conditions. His oldest child came to Christ at a church children's program, and he would come home to tell his family about Jesus. Although he had been burned by "Churchianity" as a youth in Mississippi, Perkins's heart now burned to learn more about the Jesus his son had come to know. Eventually, his blinders came off and Perkins saw that Jesus was not the white man's God but everyone's God — including his.

Sometime after Perkins converted to Christ, God started impressing on him a vision for his own people back in Mississippi (this was the Mississippi of the 1950s). Perkins told his wife that he believed God was calling him and his family to leave California and return to Mississippi to help African-Americans who were oppressed by poverty and injustice. They made that move in 1960, and they did yeomen's work in helping their people with community development. But Perkins's work did not go unnoticed by the local authorities. One night in 1970, some white police officers arrested him and dragged him inside a police station, where they beat him nearly to death. Those police officers punched and kicked him, injuring some of his vital organs, even while they put a fork in his nose and down his throat. Perkins spent the next year of his life in and out of medical care receiving treatment for the many injuries he suffered in that beating, including a heart attack.

I was privileged to be able to help bring Dr. Perkins — now an elderly man, author of several books, and an advisor to several U.S. presidents — to Portland a few years ago, where he shared his story and work at a number of venues, including Reed College. Perkins recounted his story for the Reed students the night he spoke there: he told them that, as he was lying there on that prison cell floor, looking up at those white police officers, he could not feel bitterness toward them. He could only feel pity for them. How could they hate another human being so much? Certainly something horrible had happened to each one of them that caused such hatred. Perkins then said that God called him through that traumatic ordeal to give his life to racial reconciliation.[8]

Reed College is by no means a bastion of evangelical Christianity. In fact, the Princeton Review has repeatedly listed Reed as one of the most secular colleges in America.[9] I don't know how those Reed students would have responded to Billy Graham (though I am pretty certain I know how they would have responded to Jerry Falwell). But this much I do know. Here they had come face to face with an ambassador of the crucified God, the real thing, not a figure they could easily fit into their stereotypes of evangelicals. Their response was a two-minute standing ovation for a life devoted to God, as Perkins had defined it.

John Perkins opened the eyes of those Reed students to the precious fact that at least some in the church do not deal with religion as an opiate of the masses. Perkins and his Christian Community Development As-

8. Perkins retells his story in John M. Perkins, *Let Justice Roll Down* (Ventura: Regal Books, 1976).

9. Robert Franek, with Tom Meltzer, et al., *The Best 361 Colleges: The Smart Student's Guide to Colleges,* 2006 Edition (New York: Princeton Review, 2005). The Princeton Review asks college students (more than 110,000 of them) what their schools are really like, and reports the most revealing answers in this book. Annually, Reed has maintained top rankings for academics and ignoring God. In the 2006 edition, Reed received the highest score among universities for "ignoring God on a regular basis."

sociation — based on the concepts of relocation, reconciliation, and re-distribution, coupling conversion and personal transformation before God with the conversion of social structures — are all about human liberation. And Perkins longs for God to open the eyes of the evangelical church today so that it might become truly concerned about reconciliation and human liberation here in America. Perkins's 1982 challenge to the evangelical church rings loud and clear today:

> The only purpose of the gospel is to reconcile people to God and to each other. A gospel that doesn't reconcile is not a Christian gospel at all. But in America it seems as if we don't believe that. We don't really believe that the proof of our discipleship is that we love one another (see John 13:35). No, we think the proof is in numbers — church attendance, decision cards. Even if our "converts" continue to hate each other, even if they will not worship with their brothers and sisters in Christ, we point to their "conversion" as evidence of the gospel's success. We have substituted a gospel of church growth for a gospel of reconciliation.
>
> And how convenient it is that our "church growth experts" tell us that homogeneous churches grow fastest! That welcome news seems to relieve us of the responsibility to overcome racial barriers in our churches. It seems to justify not bothering with breaking down racial barriers, since that would only distract us from "church growth." And so the most segregated racist institution in America, the evangelical church, racks up the numbers, declaring itself "successful," oblivious to the fact that the dismemberment of the body of Christ broadcasts to the world every day a hypocrisy as blatant as Peter's at Antioch — a living denial of the truth of the Gospel.[10]

We have been seduced by success, and we will downplay confronting race and class barriers to grow churches quickly. Many evangelical church leaders believe that the best way to multiply churches quickly is to make the members feel comfortable rather than comfort them with

---

10. John M. Perkins, *With Justice for All*, with a foreword by Chuck Colson (Ventura: Regal Books, 1982), pp. 107-8.

[handwritten: Just sit & listen. No give & take]

the cross that breaks down the divisions between God, us, and others. Churches cater to people's consumer passions of getting what they want, when they want it, and at the least perceived cost to themselves. However, the cross creates a transforming harmony, not a comfortable homogeneity of the status quo intent on preserving "moral (white middle-class) majorities."

Perkins seeks to be redemptive, but he continues to struggle with the status quo of the evangelical movement and its offense to African-American Christians. Charles Marsh says:

> There remain too many habits and ideas in the culture that offend black Christians. Why did such "brothers in Christ" as Jerry Falwell and Pat Robertson vehemently oppose a national holiday in honor of Martin Luther King, Jr., the most influential pastor in American history, even as they heaped praise and financial support on Ronald Reagan, the only president in recent decades (other than George W. Bush) who did not go to church regularly? . . . It is no wonder black Christians look with suspicion on white Christians who say they want racial reconciliation. White evangelicals have trapped themselves into an "ideological box" — the suburban family values agenda and all its trappings — leaving them without a credible witness in the black community. In all this, Perkins has become much more sympathetic to the black church tradition.[11]

[handwritten margin note: GWB? Barosa & devout Episcopal]

Perkins has become more sympathetic to that tradition because of his concerns for social justice and reconciliation between peoples. In contrast, the dominant evangelical church culture is largely calloused toward the black church because of evangelicals' lack of intentional concern for social justice and their bondage to consumerism. The consumer-driven church culture fosters homogeneity and upward mobility, not the transforming harmony and downward mobility of the triune God that is realized in the cross and resurrection.

In the eighteenth and nineteenth centuries, evangelicalism con-

11. Charles Marsh, *The Beloved Community: How Faith Shapes Social Justice, from the Civil Rights Movement to Today* (New York: Basic Books, 2005), p. 186.

fronted the concrete consumer "trade triangle" of slavery, shipping, and sugar; today's evangelical community must confront the abstract, more subtle trade triangle of consumer Christianity, homogeneity, and upward mobility. In this book I aim toward a theologically guided sociological engagement of practical religion. In specific terms, I wish to confront the ways evangelical-consumer or niche-church Christianity fosters racial and economic divisions, and I wish to offer an alternative theological paradigm to the one that is often embraced in the evangelical subculture.

I have entitled this book *Consuming Jesus: Beyond Race and Class Divisions in a Consumer Church* for two reasons. First, the book is about consumerism and how it affects the church in reinforcing the race and class divisions of society, and how it distorts our view of Jesus and his call for our lives. Our consumerist impulses turn him into the sappy-looking Jesus on the cover of the *Willamette Week* or even Will Ferrell's eight-pound, six-ounce baby Jesus in Ricky Bobby's dinner table prayer in *Talladega Nights*. Such distorted pictures of Jesus help us in our pursuit of the American Dream, but not toward Martin Luther King's and John Perkins's dream of removing race and class divisions in the church and society.

Today we live with an updated version of segregation. Many Americans, including evangelicals, believe that race barriers and their impact on class are in the past because we no longer live under Jim Crow legislation, with its enforcement of separate living quarters, as well as separate public bathrooms and drinking fountains, based on the color of one's skin. I would counter that segregation is still a fact of life: though it is perhaps no longer based on enforced legal structures, it is based on the norms of consumer preference. Intentionally or not, many evangelical churches are guilty of setting up structures of church growth that foster segregation, such as appealing to consumer appetites and the like. We who belong to the evangelical Christian community need to eat crow — humble pie! Moreover, we in the evangelical community need to change our appetites and eating habits: we need to leave the segregated table and its consumerist bacchanalia and gather at the table of repentance and reconciliation.

At the table of repentance and reconciliation we find forgiveness and love, hope and strength to carry on, because here at the head of the table, interceding for us and providing for our needs, is the all-consuming Jesus. That brings up the second reason for my title. Being consumed by Jesus reorients us so that we can clearly see him and clearly sense his call in our lives. Jesus' all-consuming vision and prayer to remove divisions and make us all one, as he and the Father are one, should consume us. As we consume Jesus through his Word, and his body and blood through the bread and wine of the Lord's Supper, he consumes us. And as Jesus consumes us, he graces us with a nobler vision: to remove disunity from his body the church, including race and class divisions. The triune God makes it possible for us to consume and eradicate the race and class divisions in the consumer church through our participation in the all-consuming vision of Christ. There is hope!

To realize that hope, we must first expose some of evangelicalism's disorders. The first and second chapters will consider historical and contemporary patterns that foster race and class divisions along consumer lines in evangelicalism. Historically, the evangelical movement has often been consumed with taking back America, which has given rise to a disorderly and nonredemptive engagement of the broader sphere. We must investigate these historical forces and assess their impact on the movement. We must also expose how disoriented and disordered we have been and how unable we have been to visualize consumerism's fostering of race and class divisions in the current setting. We will then be in a position to make preparations for the banquet table of an all-consuming and transforming harmony. In specific terms, we will reorder our theological frame of reference and our means of engagement. Along these lines, I will speak of the theo-political vision inaugurated with Christ's atoning work: he has overturned the fallen powers and transformed and reordered the cosmic powers, providing the necessary conditions for breaking down race and class divisions in our consumer church context (chapter 3). I will then discuss the restructuring or reordering of the human heart (chapter 4), the restructuring or reordering of church polity around Scripture and the sacraments (chapter 5), and the restructuring or reordering of the church's engagement of other churches and the broader culture in the consumer age (chapter 6). Once we have gotten there, we will have arrived at the banquet table (conclusion), where we will feast on a nobler vision of patchwork quilts and church potlucks.

CHAPTER ONE

A Faulty Order: Retreating Battle Camps and Homogeneous Units

Tracing Historical Missteps

What did the late Jerry Falwell and his liberal counterparts have in common? At least on the religious and cultural surface, the Bible-believing, soul-saving, old-world, moral-mandating Rev. Falwell and his liberal counterparts were worlds apart. However, both used power politics to build moral utopias. Here's what William Willimon, a United Methodist, says about Falwell, Pat Robertson, the Religious Right — and the Religious Left:

> Pat Robertson has become Jesse Jackson. Randall Terry of the Nineties is Bill Coffin of the Sixties. And the average American knows no answer to human longing or moral deviation other than legislation. Again, I ought to know. We played this game before any Religious Right types were invited to the White House. Some time ago I told Jerry Falwell to his face that I had nothing against him except that he talked like a Methodist. A Methodist circa 1960. Jerry was not amused.[1]

Both Left and Right have missed out on identifying the church as a distinctive polis or theo-political community that engages culture in view of the

---

1. William H. Willimon, "Been There, Preached That: Today's Conservatives Sound Like Yesterday's Liberals," *Leadership: A Practical Journal for Church Leaders* 16, no. 4 (Fall 1995): 76.

cross. For both of them, hope lies in legislation. Going beyond what Willimon says, we might say that they use power politics to promote the agenda of their special-interest groups, and they build walls of separation, not bridges of redemption. They are consumed by the wrong priorities. By his own admission, Rev. Falwell's Moral Majority is back in action today on the battlefield of the culture wars as they try to make sure that President George W. Bush succeeds with his second-term "mandate."[2] Some observers may wonder why Falwell's people — supposedly rapture and retreat fundamentalist-evangelicals — would ever seek the center stage. In the end, it may be obvious that center stage was what they wanted all along.

The contemporary activism of the new Moral Majority emerges from the context of the fundamentalist-modernist conflict in North America. In this chapter I want to trace the historical development of the fundamentalist-evangelical movement in America and shed light on the movement's current direction and focus, including a discussion of how evangelical social action fares today in the consumer age and what that entails negatively for race and class divisions. In speaking of fundamentalism, evangelicalism, and the Christian Right, I refer to distinct though inseparably related strands that come together to form the variegated pattern of the conservative Protestant movement in America. While these threads are distinct and at times represent different approaches on how to engage the broader culture, they share some of the same identifying features, such as particular doctrinal emphases (including the virgin birth of Christ, a high view of Scripture's accuracy and authority, and substitutionary atonement), concern for personal conversion, and a shared history of contending against liberal Christian theology and secular humanism. On the whole, these strands would approach social problems in a similar way — from an individual, relational, antistructural perspective.[3]

---

2. Jerry Falwell, "Faith and Values Coalition: The 21st Century Moral Majority," November 10, 2004. http://www.newsmax.com/archives/articles/2004/11/10/102729.shtml (article posted November 26, 2004). The work of the Moral Majority Coalition continues on today under the leadership of Jonathan Falwell, Rev. Falwell's son. See http://www.moralmajority.us/index.php?options=com_frontpage&itemid=1 (article posted June 2, 2007).

3. Michael O. Emerson and Christian Smith, *Divided by Faith: Evangelical Religion and*

It is best to try to understand history in order to get a handle on problematic features so that we can move forward constructively and redemptively.

The Falling Out of Fundamentalism:
From Public Square to Private Cells

The recent public activism of evangelicalism is not as unprecedented as popular political commentators might portray it. Even mainstream journalists are discovering what American historians have known for some time. For example, in a special report entitled "The New Old-Time Religion," *U.S. News and World Report* writer Jay Tolson chronicles the history and present standing of evangelicalism in America. Shaped by the great American theologian Jonathan Edwards, American evangelicalism, says Tolson, "became the dominant force in American culture and politics in the 19th century and up through the early 20th. Along the way, it touched just about every major social movement, from abolitionism to Prohibition."[4] But the movement lost its position of prominence in American cultural life, beginning in the mid-nineteenth century and climaxing in the early twentieth century (Tolson, p. 38).[5] A variety of factors contributed to the loss of prominence, factors that have come to shape the contemporary efforts of evangelicals to re-engage public life over the last three decades. These factors come together in the story of fundamentalism's rise.

---

the Problem of Race in America (New York: Oxford University Press, 2000), pp. 76, 78. For an in-depth analysis of fundamentalism-evangelicalism, see George Marsden, *Fundamentalism and American Culture: The Shaping of Twentieth-Century Evangelicalism — 1870-1925* (Oxford: Oxford University Press, 1980) [hereafter page citations in parentheses in the text]; see also Marsden, *Reforming Fundamentalism: Fuller Seminary and the New Evangelicalism* (Grand Rapids: Eerdmans, 1995).

4. Jay Tolson, "The New Old-Time Religion," *U. S. News and World Report*, December 8, 2003, p. 38 [hereafter page citations in parentheses in the text].

5. Mark Noll believes evangelicalism's decline on the public stage began in the mid-nineteenth century; see Mark A. Noll, *American Evangelical Christianity: An Introduction* (Oxford: Blackwell, 2001), p. 202.

Ranging over an assortment of issues that began in the nineteenth century, including theological modernism and Darwinian science, evangelicals found themselves increasingly in a defensive posture, which eventually gave rise to the fundamentalist movement (Tolson, pp. 38, 41). Historian George Marsden points out that fundamentalism, while developing a distinct identity, could not be dissociated from older movements from which it arose (Marsden, p. 4). Fundamentalism emerged out of currents within nineteenth-century evangelicalism and has shaped evangelicalism in the twentieth century (Marsden, p. 5). Marsden defines the fundamentalist movement as "a loose, diverse, and changing federation of co-belligerents united by their fierce opposition to modernist attempts to bring Christianity into line with modern thought" (Marsden, p. 4).

I do not have enough space in this chapter to give a detailed analysis of fundamentalism's historical development, but three themes in fundamentalism account in large part for evangelicalism's loss of prominence in the early and middle parts of the twentieth century, and they were bound up with the fundamentalist-evangelical movement's privatization of spirituality, dissolution of public faith, and loss of an extensive, overarching social conscience. It may be helpful to consider these three themes as our discussion shifts in later chapters toward the theological and ecclesial development of a theo-political vision for engaging the race and class divisions that are present today in consumerist Christianity.

The themes of fundamentalism relevant for our present purposes converge in its intellectual-cultural milieu: those themes were (1) anti-intellectualism, (2) the community's antipathy toward the "social gospel," and (3) the growing influence of a millennial eschatological viewpoint on the psyche of many fundamentalist-evangelicals.[6] One finds elements of these three themes in the life and thought of the great American evangelist D. L. Moody.

According to Marsden, "Moody's contribution to emerging fundamentalism was both large and complex. Moody was a progenitor of fun-

---

6. See David O. Moberg, *The Great Reversal: Evangelism and Social Concern*, rev. ed. (Philadelphia: Lippincott, 1977), for a related discussion of the deterioration of the evangelical church's social conscience at this time.

damentalism — it could even be argued that he was its principal progenitor" (Marsden, p. 33). While the dynamism and complex positive
influence of Moody have been felt throughout the church worldwide, his
life included aspects that can illustrate those same three characteristics
of the fundamentalism that came after him. I am not speaking of
Moody's long-term intentions but of the pervasive resonance and cultural reception of him and his ideas. As a cultural icon, Moody may
serve as a window through which to view the historical backdrop of the
emergence of the movement.

It was voiced in my Seminary days 1951-1954

The Seminary as Cemetery: Anti-Intellectualism

I have sometimes heard students say they were reluctant to enter seminary because they were afraid of losing their faith there. And thus many
within the fundamentalist-evangelical movement, past and present,
have viewed the seminary as a cemetery. I believe that there are at least
two reasons for this concern. The first reason is the concern that "head
knowledge" will cancel out "heart knowledge," that is, a love for Christ
and a passion for the simple gospel message and ministry. Grassroots piety and a passion for the gospel were characteristic of Moody. Although
certain of Moody's followers were to become very influential in shaping
the theology of fundamentalism, Marsden says that Moody's "message,
aside from the constant stress on the necessity of conversion, was of the
love of God. His theology, although basically orthodox, was ambiguous
to the point of seeming not to be theology at all" (Marsden, p. 32). This
ambiguity was no doubt due in large part to Moody's efforts to make
peace for the sake of the gospel (Marsden, pp. 32-33).

Here one can see the characteristic trait that differentiated Moody
from his fundamentalist followers: his irenic and ecumenical spirit re-
sisted theological controversy. A key reason for this was that, as Marsden notes, "Moody was a pragmatic activist, determined that nothing
should stand in the way of preaching the Gospel effectively," including
theological debates (Marsden, p. 33). Moody's key role in the formation
of the fundamentalist movement, including his charitable spirit and emphasis on evangelism, implies that fundamentalism "was always a sub-

species of the larger revivalist movement" (Marsden, pp. 38-39). While Moody's breadth of spirit is praiseworthy, his singular emphasis on evangelism may well have encouraged a lack of theological depth and engagement on the part of some of his revivalist followers. Mark Noll puts it this way: "The evangelical ethos is activistic, populist, pragmatic, and utilitarian. It allows little space for broader or deeper intellectual effort because it is dominated by the urgencies of the moment."[7] That description fits Moody and his "descendants" well.

The second reason that many within the fundamentalist-evangelical heritage see the seminary as a cemetery arises from historical fundamentalist concerns about "modernist theology" in denominational seminaries and an intensifying antagonism to views differing from the five "fundamentals of the faith," as they were known. Those five "fundamentals" were: the inerrancy of the Bible, Christ's virgin birth, Christ's substitutionary atoning work, Christ's bodily resurrection, and the historicity of Christ's miracles (later to be replaced by an emphasis on premillennialism). Along with the five "fundamentals" came a singular emphasis on the Bible as the sole basis for a curriculum, which disregarded contributions from theology (i.e., nondispensational theology), philosophy, and the like. Fundamentalism would not say that all truth is God's truth.

Things came to a head with the Scopes "Monkey Trial" in 1925. As Marsden says, "It would be difficult to overestimate the impact" of this trial "in transforming fundamentalism" (Marsden, p. 184). The fundamentalists' cultural loss to the evolutionists, modernity, and liberal theology led to a seismic shift and a volatile reaction. During the 1930s fundamentalists abandoned their mainline denominations and the denominational seminaries in droves to found independent Bible churches and Bible institutes. They wanted freedom from mainline church *structures*, infused as these institutions were with modernism. And how did these denominations become liberal? Fundamentalists placed the blame squarely on the denominational seminaries. The Bible institute movement came to serve as an alternative to seminary education in the minds of many: these new

---

7. Mark A. Noll, *The Scandal of the Evangelical Mind* (Grand Rapids: Eerdmans, 1994), p. 12.

schools offered terminal degrees that could lead to placement in the independent church network.

However, not only were the fundamentalists leaving modernism behind; they were also leaving modern education and culture behind. In exiting the denominational seminaries in massive numbers, they were also abandoning the universities to which those seminaries were joined. Dispensational theology, with which most of these churches and schools were now associated, not only championed a biblical hermeneutic of discontinuity and separation; it was also used at times to champion detachment and disengagement from the broader cultural sphere in terms of learning and life. The influences for this shift toward anti-intellectualism were as much cultural as they were religious.[8] I will say more about these cultural trends when I discuss rapture theory below. But now I wish to focus attention on fundamentalism and social activism, beginning once again with fundamentalism's forefather, Dwight Moody.

Savior of the Soul and Trickle-Down Social Ethics:
Antipathy to Social Engagement

Moody's revivalist orientation also had an impact on the broader evangelical culture concerning issues of social justice (Marsden, p. 36). To Moody, social activism, like theological debate, "threatened to distract from his primary concern for evangelism," and nothing was to stand in the way of evangelistic outreach. This disregard for social activism was a shift from Moody's early ministry, where he combined proclamation and care for the poor (Marsden, pp. 36-37). He traces the shift and gives the rationale in the following statement:

8. Marsden contends that although dispensationalist views were used at times as "rationales" to suppress social action in the fundamentalist movement, this was not a uniform practice. See Marsden, *Fundamentalism and American Culture*, p. 90. It is worth noting Shailer Mathews's point set forth in Marsden's work, namely, that the main difference between modernism and fundamentalism was not divergent responses to religious matters, but rather varying responses to modern culture. See Marsden, p. 185.

19

> When I was at work in the City Relief Society, before the [Chicago] fire, I used to go to a poor sinner with the Bible in one hand and a loaf of bread in the other. . . . My idea was that I could open a poor man's heart by giving him a load of wood or a ton of coal when the winter was coming on, but I soon found out that he wasn't any more interested in the Gospel on that account. Instead of thinking how he could come to Christ, he was thinking how long it would be before he got another load of wood. If I had the Bible in one hand and a loaf [of bread] in the other the people always looked first at the loaf; and that was just contrary to the order laid down in the Gospel.[9]

Not only was this way of thinking a shift from the early Moody; but it also stood in marked contrast to the dominant model of the evangelical church of the earlier part of the nineteenth century (Marsden, p. 37). Many earlier evangelicals had viewed social reform as effective only in the context of revival and the transformation of hearts; nonetheless, revivalism and social reform went hand in hand. Marsden says:

> The assumption that Christianity was the only basis for a healthy civilization was basic to evangelical thinking — as essential as the belief that souls must be saved for the life to come. Virtue among the citizenry, as almost all political economists said, was the foundation of successful civilization, especially a republican civilization (p. 12).

Moody's move away from social activism paralleled his decision to emphasize certain vices, such as using public transportation on Sundays or going to the theater (Marsden, p. 35). To use Tolson's term to describe fundamentalism, Moody's later emphasis was "hypermoralistic" (Tolson, p. 41).

Moody did not lack compassion; he simply believed that evangelism was the most effective way to address social concerns. This is what I refer to as "trickle-down social ethics": that is, by changing hearts we will eventually be able to change the world. Jesus is changing the world "one life at a

---

9. Moody is quoted in W. H. Daniels, ed., *Moody: His Words, Work, and Workers* (New York: Nelson & Phillips, 1877), pp. 431-32.

time." According to Marsden, Moody believed that "conversion inevitably led to personal responsibility and moral uplift, qualities which the conventional wisdom said the poor most often lacked" (Marsden, p. 37). But, regardless of intentions, such a view is shortsighted and problematical.

Why is this so? While we should not discount the necessary role evangelism and regeneration play in the transformation of lives and societies, Moody's emphasis — especially when combined with hypermoralism (the "don't drink, don't chew, don't date girls who do" kind of thinking) — fails to engage social inequities adequately. Contemporary evangelicalism's nearly solitary emphasis in many quarters on "the miracle motif" (evangelism and conversion) betrays a fundamental blindness to the immoral structural realities that oppress the poor and keep them poor. The attitude seems to be, "Get poor people saved, and they will receive the necessary moral lift to pull themselves out of the poverty pit." This kind of blindness to structural realities continues to obstruct the vision of many in the evangelical church today, as the book *Divided by Faith* makes clear.[10] Marsden notes that Moody's emphases reflected the "middle-class individualism" of his day.[11] Whether or not Moody was situated in the "heyday" of American individualism, his views on social

10. See Emerson and Smith, *Divided by Faith,* cited in note 3 above.

11. Marsden, *Fundamentalism and American Culture,* p. 37. A commentator sympathetic to Moody, Lyle W. Dorsett, argues that Moody's emphasis on saving "souls rather than striving for political change" appeared "less important to social gospelers and Christian Socialists of his day than to historians and social scientists in the last sixty or seventy years who have been disturbed that he did not devote his life to what they have perceived as a clear-cut class struggle." Lyle W. Dorsett, *A Passion for Souls: The Life of D. L. Moody,* foreword by Joseph Stowell (Chicago: Moody Press, 1997), p. 409. Dorsett's analysis of the factors shaping Moody's soul-saving framework differs from Marsden's discussion. But Dorsett does not really challenge Marsden's claim that Moody's middle-class context shaped Moody. Dorsett says: "Marsden . . . is much more balanced in his view of Moody [than other commentators], but he sees Moody's social views as primarily a product of his American middle class, individualistic values" (p. 417). While Moody's middle-class context shaped him, it is important to note that he did reach out to all sectors of society. See Thomas E. Corts's discussion of class and race in "Payment on Account," in *Mr. Moody and the Evangelical Tradition,* ed. Timothy George (London: T&T Clark International, 2004), pp. 62-66.

engagement may owe as much to American culture's influence on his thinking as they do to his reading of the Bible and his regard for "Christian" values (Marsden, p. 37). The same can be said about many evangelicals in present-day American culture.

Above and beyond Moody and his followers' singular concern for evangelism and revival, the eventual fundamentalist response to the "social gospel" movement did more than anything to negate the earlier evangelical emphasis on social activism. This factor is a key to understanding what David Moberg calls the "Great Reversal" — the radical disintegration of evangelical social concern at the beginning of the twentieth century.[12] In the imaginations of many fundamentalists, their exclusive emphasis would come to rest on Jesus as savior of the soul, and that emphasis led to a disregard of Jesus as savior of the body and cosmos as well.

That disregard was due in large part to fundamentalist fears of rival notions of Jesus as "moral teacher" and "great care giver." For example, fundamentalists were very wary of the social gospel movement as it was classically expressed by Walter Rauschenbusch: "Religious morality" is "the only thing God cares about."[13] As Rauschenbusch saw it, faith and doctrine are only significant when they serve the aims of social activism. Key promoters of the social gospel also showed the stark contrast between their views and those within the fundamentalist-evangelical movement who espoused "individualist soul-saving evangelicalism" and premillennialist views. As a result, fledgling fundamentalists who were looking to show a connection between an emphasis on social activism and the seeds of liberalism found ammunition for their own claims in their opponents' attacks. Many within the fundamentalist movement were no doubt concerned about falling victim to "guilt by association": that is, one could easily be charged with going down the path of liberalism by showing signs of a social consciousness and conscience. Fundamentalist critics of social activism could make use of the social gospel as ammunition for their "slippery-slope" claim that social activism leads to liberalism (Marsden, p. 92).

12. See Moberg, *The Great Reversal.*

13. Walter Rauschenbusch, *Christianity and the Social Crisis,* ed. Robert D. Cross (1907; reprint, New York: Macmillan, 1964), p. 6.

As the conflict accelerated, "the position that one could have both revivalism and social action became increasingly cumbersome to defend. In any case this attempt at balance declined in proportion to the increase of strident anti-modernism" (Marsden, p. 92). Moreover, the new fundamentalists simply forgot the earlier successes by evangelicals who were concerned with progressive social policies. But, as Marsden notes, the fundamentalist reaction did not spell an apolitical orientation or the abandonment of social policies but rather a fixation on conservative middle-class American social values common around the time just prior to the great controversy's emergence (Marsden, p. 93). (As a friend of mine once remarked, it is ironic that a "fixation" on 1950s mores and 1980s economics plagues many evangelical activists today.) All things considered, though, the fundamentalist reaction to the social gospel movement overshadowed and overwhelmed the classic evangelical understanding of the gospel, which involved spiritual renewal and social reform.

Although "social gospels" that reduce Christian faith to social action by making faith a predicate of activism are clearly problematical, so are those versions of the Christian faith that fail to see the gospel as social. The good news of Jesus Christ orders and reorders the whole of life. Thus I find it tragic that many in the fundamentalist-evangelical movement reacted to the social gospel by abandoning concerns for social responsibility in the public sphere. Since they believed that proponents of the social gospel were interpreting and applying the Bible exclusively in a social — or philanthropic — way (i.e., caring for the poor), fundamentalists reacted by bracketing off such concerns. But there is more to the story. This brief survey of the rise of fundamentalism and the demise of a social conscience would not be complete if we did not consider eschatology.

Rapture and Retreat: Tendencies of Premillennial Eschatology

The reaction against the social gospel movement was most likely the chief cause for the virtual disappearance of concern for social justice among fundamentalists. Yet premillennialism (at least in certain forms), as it was adopted and used in particular ways by Moody and his followers, could also reinforce the disparagement of social activism. It may prove useful to examine two of the founding figures of Wheaton College, one of evangelicalism's premiere schools, to illustrate the impact that premillennial thought could have on questions of social activism and culture.

Jonathan Blanchard, the founding president of Wheaton College, was an evangelical "social reformer"; he was also a postmillennialist. However, his son Charles was indelibly influenced by "the Moody forces," and under their influence Charles led Wheaton into a new era of fundamentalism. Crucial to this redirection was Charles's conversion to dispensational premillennialism, a perspective that often promotes a pessimistic view of engaging culture because it anticipates a rapture of the church prior to the Great Tribulation destined to fall upon the earth (Marsden, p. 31). The differences between the Blanchards, father and son, symbolize the shift in the evangelical psyche at this time. Marsden portrays the contrast this way: whereas the elder Blanchard had sought to "transform the culture," the younger Blanchard sought to separate from it. "Jonathan Blanchard had been a Puritan exhorting America to become Zion; Charles was a Puritan in an American Babylon" (Marsden, p. 32).

The pre-Tribulation rapture theory can nurture the ethos of a community on the retreat. Although it is difficult to determine a historical or logical connection, one can understand how such a link might develop. As Martin Luther might have put it, the elder Blanchard would have planted a tree today if he knew the world was going to end tomorrow. On the other hand, some dispensationalists have figured that they might as well let the world go to hell in a handbasket.[14] Why? Because everything is going to burn in the end anyway. With that perspective, Christians should stick to saving souls for heaven rather than expending our efforts to mend a sinking ship. As Dwight Moody would say, "I look

14. One interesting and positive development is that some dispensationalists are growing in their concern to bring dispensational theology to bear constructively on engaging larger social and cultural issues. See Craig A. Blaising and Darrell L. Bock, *Progressive Dispensationalism* (Wheaton: BridgePoint, 1993), p. 56.

CHAPTER TWO

Disordered Vision:
Battling the Consumer Balrog

Exposing Powers of Darkness Disguised as Angels of Light

At the close of *Fundamentalism and American Culture*, George Marsden says:

> I find that a Christian view of history is clarified if one considers real-
> ity as more or less like the world portrayed in the works of J. R. R.
> Tolkien. We live in the midst of contests between great and mysteri-
> ous spiritual forces, which we understand only imperfectly and
> whose true dimensions we only occasionally glimpse. Yet, frail as we
> are, we do play a role in this history, on the side either of the powers of
> light or of the powers of darkness. It is crucially important then, that,
> by God's grace, we keep our wits about us and discern the vast differ-
> ence between the real forces for good and the powers of darkness dis-
> guised as angels of light.[1]

In *The Lord of the Rings*, seemingly omnipresent and omnipotent forces of
wickedness were at work in Middle Earth, from the Balrog to Sauron,
leading Frodo and his companions to the point of losing their wits. Similar sinister forces are at work today, and they have an impact on the
church and broader culture to their very core, which sometimes leads us
to lose our wits and discernment.

1. George M. Marsden, *Fundamentalism and American Culture: The Shaping of Twentieth-Century Evangelicalism, 1870-1925* (Oxford: Oxford University Press, 1980), pp. 229-30.

One of the forces Tolkien subtly depicts in his masterful trilogy is industrialization's onslaught and the resulting depersonalization and dehumanization of the world. Parallel forces that have an impact on the evangelical church and culture at large today are consumerism and the free-market enterprise. The consumerist mindset entails giving consumers what they want, when they want it, and at the least cost to consumers themselves. It also creates in consumers the desire to want, and then to want more, even to want things they did not originally want — programming them to buy a given product in the free-market system.[2] Such catering to what consumers want and creating wants in order to win them over to buying a given product is socially acceptable today, even in the church.

The consumerist, free-market spirit disguises itself as an angel of light. However, it cleverly shapes race and class divisions in the evangelical church and beyond, and it makes conquering these depersonalizing and dehumanizing forces increasingly difficult. People tend to associate with those with whom they feel most comfortable. Birds of a certain socioeconomic feather flock together. In a free-market church culture, those who cater most to this consumer force thrive best. It all appears to be benign; yet it is very divisive. It divides churches along the lines of race and class. A church movement given to pragmatic impulses — targeting predominantly white, suburban, and exurban middle-class groups with conservative social mores in order to grow churches quickly — will hardly be able to withstand such forces. In fact, such a movement provides a wonderful breeding ground in which these forces can flourish and thrive.[3] In this chapter I will analyze the subtle power of

2. In an article in *Newsweek,* John Kenneth Galbraith claimed that "the modern economy didn't flourish by satisfying the needs of consumers, but by creating the desire for products consumers didn't need at all." Galbraith, "Honestly — You Shouldn't Have: Stuff and Stuff and Nonsense," *Newsweek,* Dec. 3, 2001, p. 76.

3. A 2005 *New York Times Magazine* article on a megachurch in Surprise, Arizona, claims that, as with "many fast-growing exurbs," the typical Surprise resident "is a young, white, married couple of modest means. These are people that the Republican Party has always run well with — its conventional wisdom among political analysts that young, middle-class couples raising children tend to be conservative — and in 2004 the G.O.P. made a strong play for exurbanites. Megachurches were a key part of

consumerism — the presumed angel of light — and how it negatively shapes people's thinking and acting concerning issues such as race and class, most notably in the evangelical church. I will focus on exposing some of the reasons why the American evangelical church is often blind to the "trade triangle" of the present day: consumerism, upward mobility, and homogeneity in the church.

Exposing the Church's Blindness to the Consumer Trade Triangle

It is very difficult for American evangelicals to understand and go from a glimpse to a conceptual grasp of the ever-present and diabolical forces of that trade triangle. There are multiple reasons for such a conceptual blindness. We have a hard time seeing how catering to consumerism can promote race and race-related class divisions. As Americans, many of us evangelicals believe that race and class problems are behind us, that consumerism and the free market are basically benign, and that catering to people's desires is good if the church wishes to grow and be successful.

Blind to Ever-Evolving Racialization

One of the reasons it is difficult for American evangelicals to grasp the impact of these forces is that they are first of all American, and many in America tend to see racialization in terms of "constants" rather than "variables," as Michael Emerson and Christian Smith point out. In other words, Americans tend to attach racialization to a particular era, not realizing that racialization adapts and evolves with time. The failure to recognize the evolving nature of racialization has "grave implications": the more people ignore racialization or think that it is behind them, the further entrenched it becomes.[4]

---

the strategy." Jonathan Mahler, "The Soul of the New Exurb," *The New York Times Magazine,* Mar. 27, 2005, p. 37.

4. Michael O. Emerson and Christian Smith, *Divided by Faith: Evangelical Religion*

Racialization is a constant reality that has an impact on every area of life, from economics to politics to education to "social" and "religious systems" (E-S, p. 170). Emerson and Smith define a racialized society in the following terms: "[A] racialized society is *a society wherein race matters profoundly for differences in life experiences, life opportunities, and social relationships*." They add that "a racialized society can also be said to be 'a society that allocates different economic, political, social, and even psychological rewards to groups along racial lines, lines that are socially constructed'" (E-S, p. 7).[5]

Many believe that racialization is no longer an issue because African-Americans no longer live under Jim Crow laws, which put them at the back of the bus and made them drink from different fountains and go to different schools (E-S, pp. 8-9, 90). Jim Crow legislation, like slavery, may be a thing of the past, but racialization and classism are not; they simply take new forms under the laws of consumer preference.

It should not be surprising to us that these issues persist. As the movie *Crash* illustrates dramatically, we are suspicious and fearful of "the other" — black, white, Hispanic, Asian, Middle Eastern, and so forth. We have to deal with our suspicions and fears whenever we crash into "the other" at the intersections of our overhyped American-melting-pot freeways and byways. We often seek to gain an advantage over others or reinforce the metal doors and glass windows of separation between us when we crash. One way we seek to gain an advantage and/or reinforce boundaries is by valuing or devaluing people according to the color of their skin or the color of their credit cards, enslaving their humanity in reductionist conceptual prisons in a not-so-free-market society.

---

and the Problem of Race in America (New York: Oxford University Press, 2000), p. 8 [hereafter cited as E-S with page references in parentheses in the text].

5. The quotation is taken from Eduardo Bonilla-Silva and Amanda Lewis, "The 'New Racism': Toward an Analysis of the U.S. Racial Structure, 1960s-1990s," unpublished manuscript, 1997, p. 474.

Blind to Omnipresent Consumer-Market Forces

Not only is it difficult for American evangelicals to grasp racialization; often, as Americans, we fail to grasp how evil and dehumanizing the consumer-market forces can be. We tend to see the market forces and consumerism as benign and basic to our existence — even beautiful. Gordon Bigelow says this about the market:

> Economics, as channeled by its popular avatars in media and politics, is the cosmology and the theodicy of our contemporary culture. More than religion itself, more than literature, more than cable television, it is economics that offers the dominant creation narrative of our society, depicting the relation of each of us to the universe we inhabit, the relation of human beings to God. And the story it tells is a marvelous one. In it an enormous multitude of strangers, all individuals, all striving alone, are nevertheless all bound together in a beautiful and natural pattern of existence: the market. This understanding of markets — not as artifacts of human civilization but as phenomena of nature — now serves as the unquestioned foundation of nearly all political and social debate.[6]

Whether or not it is self-evident that all people are created equal, it is self-evident to many today that all people are created to exist as solitary individuals who shop and sell.

By no means benign and beautiful, this consumer-market orientation depersonalizes and dehumanizes us. Don Slater speaks of the problematical features of "consumer culture" in a market system: "Consumer culture denotes a social arrangement in which the relation between lived culture and social resources, between meaningful ways of life and the symbolic and material resources on which they depend, is mediated through markets." Moreover, Slater claims:

> Consumer culture is about continuous self-creation through the accessibility of things which are themselves presented as new, modish,

6. Gordon Bigelow, "Let There Be Markets: The Evangelical Roots of Economics," *Harper's* 310, no. 1860 (May 2005): 33.

43

faddish or fashionable, always improved and improving. In keeping with the fashionable experience it provides, the very idea of consumer culture is constantly heralded as new: in each generation the Columbuses of capitalism rediscover the promised land of affluent freedom; while critics — both left and right — report our arrival in a frozen land of wealth without value.

Slater says of consumer culture: "All social relations, activities and objects can in principle be exchanged as commodities. This is one of the most profound secularizations enacted by the modern world." The "potential for any thing, activity or experience to be commodified or to be replaced by commodities perpetually places the intimate world of the everyday into the impersonal world of the market and its values." Moreover, consumer freedom becomes "compulsory" since it serves to nourish and sustain the "social relations and identities" of daily existence.[7]

R. Kendall Soulen and Jonathan Sacks also weigh in on the problem of consumer and market forces. Soulen says:

> The market . . . promises to make the consumer king, and encourages us to think that we are in charge. But the market charges a high price in return, namely, the increasing commodification of human life itself. To take just one example, as genetic knowledge becomes more complete and available to consumers through law, prospective parents will be subject to pressure to screen their pregnancies in order to screen out inefficiencies such as mental retardation, genetic disorders, etc.[8]

Sacks, the chief rabbi of the United Hebrew Congregations of the British Commonwealth, says:

7. Don Slater, *Consumer Culture and Modernity* (Cambridge: Polity, 1997), pp. 8, 10, 27. See also Vincent J. Miller, *Consuming Religion: Christian Faith and Practice in a Consumer Culture* (New York: Continuum, 2003), for a detailed analysis of consumerism and its impact on the church and broader culture.

8. R. Kendall Soulen, "'Go Tell Pharaoh,' Or, Why Empires Prefer a Nameless God," *Cultural Encounters: A Journal for the Theology of Culture* 1, no. 2 (Summer 2005): 54-56.

The fatal conceit for Judaism is to believe that the market governs the totality of our lives, when it in fact governs only a limited part of it, that which concerns the goods we think of as being subject to production and exchange. There are things fundamental to being human that we do not produce; instead we receive from those who came before us and from God Himself. And there are things that we may not exchange, however high the price.[9]

Slater, Soulen, and Sacks are not alone. A growing number of scholars are speaking of the devastating effects of a market worldview for human life, not to mention religious and ecclesial life. Philip Kenneson and James Street contend that the market mind-set of exchanging values in the church is selling out the church: the market mind-set means that the gospel signifies an exchange between God and us rooted in satisfying our untrained needs. Countering this frame of reference, they claim that the gospel always remains God's gift to us.[10]

Race and class divisions often go together because race and income tend to track one another in the United States. And, as Emerson and Smith show, racialization has an impact on all areas of life, including income and healthcare (E-S, p. 7). In this light, one might argue that there is and will be diversity in the church to the extent that people of different ethnicities meet one another at the same economic level. If so, one might be led to claim that the current market system can help overcome the racial divide, qualifying this by adding that greater sensitivity and structural charity and solidarity are needed until equality becomes a reality. However, even if market equality materializes, at what cost to the community will that dream of equality come? Must it take *relational* sacrifices to the market for people from communities of racial and ethnic minorities to attain equal footing and unity in society, including the church? What will the cost be to the community, especially among ethnic minorities that traditionally have placed high value on family and extended fam-

9. Jonathan Sacks, "Markets and Morals," *First Things*, No. 105 (Aug./Sept. 2000): 28.

10. Philip D. Kenneson and James L. Street, *Selling Out the Church: The Dangers of Church Marketing* (Eugene: Cascade Books, 1997).

ily ties? And what is one to make of those from different classes within one's own ethnicity? How do they fit into affluent niche churches that are intentionally or unintentionally defined along class lines?

Buying power often defines value and worth today: those with more buying power are often deemed more valuable and thus can use those "less valuable" to attain even greater buying power, racializing and "classizing" them in the process in order to make this happen. Cynthia Moe-Lobeda also speaks of human value and race in terms of buying power: "Human worth is placed in relationship to buying power," where humanity is defined in terms of "homo economicus, consumens, et dominans" (the economic, consuming, and dominating creature). She illustrates this point by drawing attention to the value associated with "Euro-Americans" more successfully controlling and dominating the planet's resources than "people of color." As a result of such dominance and control, they are esteemed as being inherently more valuable and more fully human and therefore have more human rights. . . ."[11]

I agree with Moe-Lobeda's cultural analysis, but I would argue that its setting up of "Euro-Americans" and "people of color" as the two poles of oppressor-oppressed is too general; such a generalization diminishes and is harmful to the larger point of economic oppression. Economic oppression can and does transcend ethnic and racial boundaries. There are whites who oppress whites (i.e., "white trash"), even people of color who oppress whites and blacks. This is why I want to attend to race *and* class divisions in a consumerist society in this book.

We often assign value today based on need and usefulness. In a consumer-oriented, free-market society, the value of something increases when the demand for it increases; thus value is not inherent, but imposed. This is true of products, but also of people: we often treat people as commodities, not as persons in communion. Human value is based on usefulness and likability. The same holds true for churches: churches provide religious products, and their value depends on how many people are attracted to the religious goods and services they pro-

11. Cynthia D. Moe-Lobeda, *Healing a Broken World: Globalization and God* (Minneapolis: Fortress Press, 2002), p. 60.

vide. Many churches find that the best way to grow is to "target" a particular niche audience or demographic and determine what religious product best scratches that group's itch. The omnipresent and omnipotent stature of the free-market enterprise has influenced the evangelical church in how it approaches and perceives "church growth" (E-S, pp. 137-39, 150-51).

For instance, "the homogeneous-unit principle" championed by Donald McGavran and C. Peter Wagner and used by many thriving congregations across the United States is often commandeered to accommodate and complement people's affinities and likes. This principle involves the notion that churches grow most quickly and with the fewest problems when they focus on targeting homogeneous subcultures. McGavran's approach to church growth and multiethnic ministry is a bit complicated:

> Because of the intense battle against race prejudice, the concept of separate races of men is discredited in many circles. Missionaries often carry this antipathy to race into their work in tribes and castes who believe themselves to be separate races, marry within their people and have an intense racial consciousness. But to ignore the significance of race hinders Christianization. It makes an enemy of race consciousness, instead of an ally. It does no good to say that tribal peoples ought not to have race prejudice. They do have it and are proud of it. It can be understood and should be made an aid to Christianization.[12]

Yet McGavran also argues (in *Understanding Church Growth*) that the potential exists for healthy, multiethnic Christian works in diverse urban settings. In such settings, the church must be strategic in promoting multiethnic ministries: "In such cities, some supratribal churches are growing rapidly. [Here] the unifying brotherhood should be stressed, breaking

---

12. McGavran, "The Bridges of God," in *Perspectives on the World Christian Movement: A Reader*, ed. Ralph D. Winter and Steven C. Hawthorne, 3rd ed. (Pasadena: William Carey Library, 1999), p. 324. For representative works by these key figures in the church-growth movement, see the following: Donald A. McGavran, *Understanding Church Growth*, ed. C. Peter Wagner, 3rd rev. ed. (Grand Rapids: Eerdmans, 1990); C. Peter Wagner, *Our Kind of People: The Ethical Dimensions of Church Growth in America* (Atlanta: John Knox Press, 1979).

with the old homogeneous unit should become a prerequisite for baptism, and worship in the standard language should become the rule."[13]

In the context of the homogeneous-unit principle, the specialty-shop church replaces the department-store model, which would cater to *everyone's* likes and needs (E-S, pp. 139-41). Though there is a certain pragmatic assumption when the church targets a homogeneous subculture — for example, middle- and upper-middle-class conservative whites — such a mindset seems to ignore the fact that, just because something works best (and lures the lost people to use it), does not mean that it *is* best. The church may grow, but at what long-term cost to confronting race and class divisions? As Americans, evangelicals are often blind to faulty pragmatic practices because Americans rarely question success. The Germans were the same way: they were blind to diabolical evil because Hitler's program was very efficient and effective in making Germany "work" and returning it to prominence. The moral of this comparison is only that we should not be too quick to promote certain purposes just because they work and prove successful.

Blinded by Success

Many people come to church to have their needs met, and they will choose the church that best suits their tastes and the needs they perceive. It is often about satisfaction at the least cost (E-S, p. 144). The result of following through on this impulse is a sellout to the status quo and debilitates efforts to break down walls of division. The most dominant and successful leaders and movements are the proponents of the status quo. (I would add that, at best, such leaders and movements offer surface-level gestures toward racial justice, if they offer them at all.) Individuals with prophetic zeal for such issues as racial reconciliation often find themselves either marginalized or pressured to compromise their message, to water it down in order to be successful (E-S, pp. 162-66). And prophets in America are not often successful — so they usually get stoned.

13. McGavran, *Understanding Church Growth*, p. 179.

One of America's most successful pastors is Rick Warren. Now I do not believe that Warren does what he does in order to be successful. It is simply that in America, precisely because his ministry is so successful, we don't often question his paradigm; in fact, we fail to see certain problematical features. Warren is no defender of the status quo, and his recent comments and actions concerning poverty and HIV/AIDS in Africa are quite prophetic. Recounting how God began burdening his heart in 2003 for the poor in Africa, Warren says: "I found those 2,000 verses on the poor. How did I miss that? I went to Bible college, two seminaries, and I got a doctorate. How did I miss God's compassion for the poor? I was not seeing all the purposes of God. The church is the body of Christ. The hands and feet have been amputated and we're just a big mouth, known more for what we're against." With eyes wide open, Warren prayed: "God, would you use me to reattach the hands and the feet to the body of Christ, so that the whole church cares about the whole gospel in a whole new way through the local church?"[14]

But Warren's *The Purpose Driven Church* is not a prophetic book. It is important to examine Warren's work carefully and critically given that he has become iconic for many Americans inside and outside the evangelical church. He is, after all, "America's New People's Pastor."[15] While Warren is a man of personal integrity, entrepreneurial creativity, and pastoral and evangelistic zeal, his *Purpose Driven Church* model, based on McGavran's paradigm (he pays tribute to McGavran for his model of church growth and how it has served to sharpen his ministry focus in the birth and growth of Saddleback Valley Community Church[16]) caters to consumer market forces, albeit inadvertently. Two factors illustrate this orientation.

First, Warren exhorts the reader to focus on good news: "Crowds al-

14. Rick Warren, quoted in Timothy C. Morgan, "Purpose Driven in Rwanda," *Christianity Today,* Oct. 20, 2005, p. 34.

15. See David Van Biema, "The 25 Most Influential Evangelicals in America," *Time,* Feb. 7, 2005.

16. See Rick Warren, *The Purpose Driven Church: Growth Without Compromising Your Message & Mission* (Grand Rapids: Zondervan Publishing House, 1995), pp. 29-30 [hereafter page citations in parentheses in the text].

ways flock to hear good news. There is enough bad news in the world that the last thing people need is to hear *more* bad news when they come to church" (p. 225). It is true that the gospel is good news, and thus Warren is right when he says that, "if it isn't good news, it isn't the Gospel" (p. 224). He is also correct in saying that the gospel "is the best news in the world." But why is it the best news? His answer is, in part, because it offers forgiveness, security, and acceptance, among other things (pp. 224-25). Once again, Warren is correct. But the Good News is also costly news, and Jesus never engaged in bait and switch. As soon as Jesus began his public ministry, he was making radical claims on people's lives. True, he met those early followers where they were, and he did not expect them to become Billy Grahams overnight. But Jesus did not leave them where they were, and he called them to follow him wherever he went, even from the beginning of his call on their lives (see Matt. 4 and 5).

Warren's claim that preachers "are to speak only what benefits" the people requires clarification (p. 227). What does he mean by "benefit"? Surely, the Good News benefits people by breaking down divisions between them based on ethnicity and economics (Gal. 3:28). If the strategy is to "start where people are and move them to where you want them to be," as Warren urges the reader, will the consumer-sensitive church ever be prepared to contend against the incessant consumer impulses that lead people to shop and find the church that gives them the spiritual goods they want, that is, the goods they think benefit them — at the least cost to themselves? How beneficial will such consumers find the church's new "breaking down divisions benefits package"?[17] Many

---

17. Saddleback's "Life Development Process" educational program and its specialist service groups for service projects (such as its orphanage in Mexico and its prison ministry) certainly have the potential for turning "Yuppies" ("Young Urban Professionals") into "Yummies" ("Young Urban Missionaries"), as Warren once affectionately described his educational objective. However, those overseeing the "Life Development Process" will need to educate people on the structural forces such as the consumer ideology that hinder efforts to overcome race and class barriers, if these young urban missionaries are to achieve long-term and widespread gains. Moreover, church leaders will need to move beyond allowing small groups to specialize; these church leaders will need to make sure that they do not relegate responsibility for social engagement to

choosy church shoppers will simply pack their bags, pocketbooks, and wallets at this point and move their allegiance to the church next door. That turn of events would be better, at least, than what happened to Jesus at the outset of his public ministry: in Luke 4 (which Warren quotes in making his point about preaching the Good News [p. 224]), Jesus proclaimed the Good News to the people, and they loved what he had to say — until he confronted them over their ethnic and religious divisions (Luke 4:22-30). That "good news" moved them so much that they tried to throw him off a cliff during the altar call.

The apostle Paul's most natural and immediate inroad to connect with gentiles was to go to the synagogue, where he would find God-fearing gentiles among the Jews. However, he made it clear from the beginning that Jewish and gentile believers in Christ were on equal footing through faith in Christ. This unnatural claim did not go over well with either group in the short or the long term, which was the historical-cultural context for his writing the Epistle to the Romans. James Dunn (commenting on Rom. 1:16) says that Paul "does not for a moment forget, nor does he want his Gentile readers to forget . . . Jewish priority in God's saving purpose . . . ; but equally fundamental is his conviction that Jewish priority does not shift the 'terms of salvation' one whit beyond faith. The need to explain and defend this double emphasis is the driving force behind the whole epistle."[18]

Some may argue that Warren's baseball diamond model of the "life development process" moves people to the stage required to address social issues. Unlike Paul, though, Warren's purpose-driven church paradigm does not include the breaking down of societal divisions as a critical purpose of the gospel and church existence (see Gal. 3:28). The church must be very intentional about challenging both racial divisions and consumerist impulses at every phase of its ministry to people.

---

consumer preference, community service-specialty groups alone. Otherwise, there will be far too many "Yuppies" and far too few "Yummies." See Warren's discussion of "The Life Development Process," "Yummies," and "service groups," *Purpose Driven Church*, pp. 143-46.

18. James D. G. Dunn, *Romans 1–8*, Word Biblical Commentary, vol. 38A (Dallas: Word Books, 1988), p. 40.

Preachers must deal with problems and bad news from their pulpits — and in their ministries to their communities from the get-go. The Good News does not hide from our brokenness or hide our brokenness from us: the gospel deals with broken people and fallen conditions, and it addresses those human conditions by proclaiming Christ's transforming power. That is what makes it the Good News. Perhaps Baby Boomers do not wish to hear more bad news; but those reaching out to Generation X find that the young want to deal with their pain and brokenness — even on Sunday morning![19] The preaching and practice of a Martin Luther King, Jr., and a John Perkins do not skirt brokenness (nor do they revel in it, for that matter). Rather, their preaching and practice address our brokenness and pain in order to shape the beloved community in view of our everlasting hope: "Let justice roll down like waters and righteousness like a mighty stream!"

What kind of beloved community is Warren talking about? Or, at the very least, what might others take his unguarded statements to communicate? He speaks of the good news of acceptance laid out in the gospel. But what kind of acceptance is this? Is it the acceptance of those who look just like you, the "Saddleback Sam" living next door? He says that "Saddleback Sam is the typical unchurched man who lives in our area. His age is late thirties or early forties. He has a college degree and may have an advanced degree. (The Saddleback Valley has one of the highest household education levels in America.) He is married to Saddleback Samantha, and they have two kids, Steve and Sally." Sam not only is "well educated"; he "likes his job," and he "likes where he lives." "Health and fitness are high priorities for him and his family"; he would "rather be in a large group than a small one," "is skeptical of 'organized religion,'" "likes contemporary music," "thinks he is enjoying life more than he did five years ago," "is satisfied, even smug, about his station in life," "prefers the casual and informal over the formal," and "is overextended in both time and money" (pp. 169-70).

Warren encourages the reader to target according to wants and

19. See Rick McKinley's book, *This Beautiful Mess: Practicing the Presence of the Kingdom of God* (Sisters, OR: Multnomah Press, 2006).

likes. For example, he tells the reader to target the "typical unchurched person your church wants to reach" (p. 169, in the chapter entitled "Who Is Your Target?"). As your church reaches out to that typical unchurched person, it will probably be targeting those of your own affinity group. Warren offers demographic data on Saddleback Sam (pp. 169-71). One way to read this is that the church should go after those whom they want to reach, all the while appealing to what their target audience wants.

Demographic targeting is not the same as deliberate contextualization. "Targeting" as cultivating intentional contact is basically benign; but "targeting" as a marketing strategy is problematic. The set of practices built into demography militate against whole-person and whole-community analysis. In contrast, contextualization (as I am using it here) involves thick description and life-on-life involvement from one person to another person in a given community, and it accounts for sensitivity to that community's language and location. Church leaders should contextualize their outreach in terms of language and location — but not according to "likings." (My point about language is not intended to denigrate the fine work of those who provide bi- and trilingual services for their church families.) I would hate to be the person attending a purpose-driven church who comes to the realization that he is not the kind of person that church is targeting. The fact that my likings are different might very well mean that the church might not really like me. And there is another question: Do the purpose-driven kinds of churches *intentionally* make room in their pews or their auditorium seating for migrant farmers or motel maids from Mexico?

A church that caters to satisfying untrained needs by nurturing and appealing to affinity groupings of well-trained connoisseurs perpetuates race and class divisions. C. S. Lewis weighs in on the matter. In *The Screwtape Letters,* Lewis's account of fallen human life and action today, the demon Screwtape instructs his young nephew, Wormwood, that if he cannot keep his patient from attending church, he should coax him into becoming a church shopper, ever in search of "the church that 'suits' him," turning him into a "taster or connoisseur of churches," a "critic" (instead of a "pupil"). Screwtape promotes the affinity-based and niche-based model of church life and growth. According to him, congregationally modeled churches turn churches into clubs, perhaps ultimately factions. In contrast to Screwtape and Wormwood, Lewis contends that churches should emphasize a "unity of place" — not a unity of "likings" — and should bring "people of different classes and psychology together in the kind of unity" that the demons' enemy — God — desires.[20]

Warren says, "You'll best reach those you relate to," and "as a leader you'll attract who you are, not who you want" (p. 176), though earlier he encourages the reader to target "the typical unchurched person your church wants to reach," as noted above. While Warren thinks that it is *possible* to reach people who are different from oneself, it is not as *sensible*. Those who have the "missionary gift" are exceptions to the rule, and Warren points to the apostle Paul as such an exception (pp. 176-77). The same would have to be true of Peter, of course, who reached Samaritans and gentiles (Acts 8 and 10), and of Jesus himself, who ministered to tax collectors, prostitutes, zealots, Samaritans, Canaanites, and the list could go on — though reaching out to any of those kinds of groups today would turn the stomachs of some in the church. If the three most visible evangelists in the New Testament are all exceptions to the "evangelism" rule, where do we turn to find the New Testament norm to follow?

Rick Warren reflects the populist orientation of many evangelicals. The movement is close to popular culture and adapts itself well to new pop culture trends. But its tendency to allow that American culture — including consumer culture — to shape its forms can also bring about a change in its fundamental message and outreach. The church must certainly do its very best to make the gospel understandable, though not *comfortable*, which would take away the offense of the gospel. In our effort to make the gospel relevant to the Saddleback Sams and Samanthas, making them feel comfortable so that we can deliver the gospel goods, we are often tempted to take away the gospel's offense. This, in turn, makes it difficult to take the offensive on such things as race and class divisions — at least in the short term.

René Descartes's dictum "I think, therefore I am" dominated the

---

20. C. S. Lewis, *The Screwtape Letters*, with *Screwtape Proposes a Toast*, rev. ed. (New York: Macmillan Publishing Company, 1982), pp. 72-73.

mind of modernity (from the sixteenth century). "I shop at Wal-Mart, therefore I am" dominates the contemporary American mind and imagination. *Homo sapiens* (the wise and thinking creature) has evolved into *homo economicus* (the economic creature), to the point of becoming *homo consumens* (the consuming creature).[21] We live in the age of consumer culture, the grand supermarket or shopping mall of desire, and many progressive, culture-engaging churches have unwittingly taken the bait — hook, line, and sinker.

Blind to Evangelical Social Structures

INDIVIDUAL-RELATIONAL BASIS   Not only are we evangelicals often blind to consumerism's impact on race and class divisions because we are American; we are also blind to it because we are American *evangelicals*. As American evangelicals, we prize the individual and personal relationships and we highlight the need for personal and friendship evangelism. These values are significant emphases in themselves. The Bible has much to say about the importance of the individual, personal responsibility, and the need for evangelism. However, when these values are coupled with a pragmatic (anti-intellectual) antipathy toward social engagement and an antistructural bent, they become unbalanced: Do whatever it takes to get people saved. . . . Save and ask questions later. . . . Jesus is changing the world one person at a time. . . . The message is that, if we focus on building personal relationships, social-structural problems such as racialization will eventually take care of themselves.

As evangelicals, we often define success in terms of getting people into a saving relationship with Jesus Christ regardless of the method we use or the long-term consequences of using them — such as the homogeneous-unit principle. The following quotation from Bill Hybels,

21. See Moe-Lobeda, *Healing a Broken World*, p. 59, for her discussion of both phrases, and for the use of the phrase *homo economicus* in discussing "neo-classical economic theory." Although one may distinguish between two eras, one dominated by reason and the other dominated by economics and the like, one cannot separate them, for as Moe-Lobeda argues, "rational thought is the highest form of humanness, and self-interested economic activity is the highest form of rationality . . ." (p. 52).

senior pastor of Willow Creek Community Church, illustrates these problems:

> Willow Creek started in the era when, as the book [*United by Faith*] noted, the church growth people were saying, "Don't dissipate any of your energies fighting race issues. Focus everything on evangelism." It was the homogeneous unit principle of church growth. And I remember as a young pastor thinking, *That's true.* I didn't know whether I wanted to chance alienating people who were seekers, whose eternity was on the line, and who might only come to church one time. I wanted to take away as many obstacles as possible, other than the Cross, to help people focus on the gospel.
>
> So now, 30 years later, as I read this book, I recognize that a true biblical functioning community must include being multi-ethnic. My heart beats so fast for that vision today. I marvel at how naïve and pragmatic I was 30 years ago.[22]

While not wishing to remove the obstacle of the Cross, Hybels's unwillingness to cross the race divide at Willow Creek meant that he reinforced racial divisions in church culture. When one takes the noble aim of reaching the lost and excludes considering such issues as racial divisions because of pragmatic concerns (i.e., getting people saved no matter what), such exclusive focus reinforces homogeneity, awards complacency, and becomes reductionist (i.e., it focuses on getting some people saved to the exclusion of others).

Hybels started Willow Creek with the noble ambition of communicating the gospel to his generation, realizing that traditional churches and churchly forms were structured in ways that failed to communicate to the lost. Therefore, he and others set out to restructure the church and its life. However, in their efforts to reach the lost, they also unwittingly structured their church in a negative way. Hybels's aim to reach a particular homogeneous target audience of seekers, once it was given *primacy*, became malignant. It kept him from seeking to break down the race di-

---

22. Bill Hybels, quoted in Edward Gilbreath and Mark Galli, "Harder than Anyone Can Imagine," *Christianity Today*, April 2005, p. 38.

vide. By refusing to move beyond homogeneity in their efforts to reach a certain niche group of lost consumers, Hybels and company became blind to the fact that they were keeping themselves from reaching many more kinds of lost consumers for the all-consuming Christ.

The fact that Hybels is now alert to the problematical nature of certain past practices is a cause for rejoicing, especially given the profound impact his ministry has had on many churches.[23] If someone of Hybels's stature has made public confession, isn't the battle won? Why spill more ink? Can't we all go home now? I wish the battle were won and that we could all go home. But the problem runs deeper than the homogeneous-unit principle, and it runs deeper than the personal influence of notable evangelical leaders. Some admirers will no doubt follow Bill Hybels's lead in expressing regret and remorse for having used the homogeneous-unit principle for church growth on American soil. Yet I fear that, even as they switch to pursuing a multiethnic ministry in their quest to reach lost souls and make churches grow, they do not question the prevalent pragmatic consumerist mind-set. What happens if and when "multiethnic" loses its appeal and people no longer crave multiethnic goods and services? Will they go back to using the homogeneous-unit principle? We American evangelicals need to move beyond our pragmatic orientation and short-term vision of focusing almost exclusively on building personal relationships with individuals to win them for Christ. An unguarded strength becomes a glaring and grave weakness when we fail to contend against problematical structures that divide people along race

23. Hybels claims that the book *United by Faith* has had a profound influence on him. Curtiss Paul DeYoung, Michael O. Emerson, George Yancey, and Karen Chai Kim, *United by Faith: The Multiracial Congregation as an Answer to the Problem of Race* (Oxford: Oxford University Press, 2003). Not only has Hybels realized the problematical nature of certain practices, but he is also educating fellow Christian leaders on the need to become more holistic in their outreach. I find it most encouraging that Hybels is addressing race and related social issues at Willow Creek's influential Leadership Summits. Refer to Bill Hybels, *The Leader's Edge*, Aug. 9, 2001 (©2003, Seeds Audio Ministry, A Ministry of Willow Creek Community Church) for a sample of his engagement of the race question. The talk was presented at the 2001 Leadership Summit; the 2006 Leadership Summit addressed HIV/AIDS in Africa.

and class lines. And such a failure has long-term consequences for reaching people who are different from us for Christ. But our individual-relational basis is not the only problem. Evangelicals are often anti-structural in orientation, and that also blinds us to addressing race and class divisions.

ANTISTRUCTURAL BIAS   Emerson and Smith claim that most white American evangelicals approach the race problem in light of free-will individualism and relationalism, while they reject "structural explanations" (E-S, pp. 76, 78). This antistructural orientation reveals a lack of proper awareness — the absence of a key tool or tools for remedying racialization in America, especially within the Christian church (E-S, p. 78). They claim that many white evangelicals are suspicious of structural solutions because they often view sin and conversion along individualistic lines. Moreover, evangelicals often view conversion as a cure-all — "get everyone converted and all our problems, including racialization, will eventually disappear" — an outlook the authors call "the miracle motif." Thus individualism and the miracle motif conspire to hamper white evangelical responses to racial divisions.

About this narrow focus, Mark Noll says:

> At its best, the evangelical desire to rescue the perishing has meant putting the perishing on their feet in the here and now as well as preparing them for eternity. Of course, we evangelicals are often not at our best, so the occasions are many of having been lured away from Christ-inspired social service by prejudice, class-consciousness, middle-class fastidiousness, blindness to the structural conditions of power that condition personal choices, and the many other forms of social sinfulness that beset the human race in general.[24]

As a committed evangelical, Noll applauds the evangelical desire to rescue the perishing. But it must involve holistic outreach. He would no doubt agree with Emerson and Smith, who recognize that the evangeli-

24. Mark A. Noll, *American Evangelical Christianity: An Introduction* (Oxford: Blackwell Publishers, Ltd., 2001), p. 276.

cal emphasis on personal relationships, repentance, and reconciliation may prove to be vital components in addressing the matter at hand, as well as their claim that a solely structural response to the problem would likely be equally naïve (E-S, p. 170). A multifaceted approach is needed. As I have observed above, an unguarded strength — no matter the tradition — can become a glaring and grave weakness.

White evangelicals whose social networks include minorities are more sensitive to the complexity of the issues, and thus they are suspicious of quick-fix relational solutions. John Perkins has a classic baseball analogy on this subject. Two teams have been playing baseball. After seven innings, it comes out that the team that is ahead has been cheating the whole game: as a result, the score is 20 to 0. This team makes apologies, but they don't change the score going into the final two innings. Obviously, the team that is down 20-0 is still in an unfair, severely disadvantaged position. And thus it is with the racialized game being played between whites and blacks. A history of disadvantage does carry over into the present. And the situation is far too complex to attempt to alleviate the problem in the way that some white evangelical Christians would like to, namely, to confess and to seek to build relationships with African-Americans without addressing structural issues of disadvantage: "The legacy is there," says an interviewee of Emerson and Smith. "So it's not an 'I forgive you' and it's done. It's just too complex for that. It's gotta be a lifetime process" (E-S, p. 127).

People often have such things as red-lining (the refusal to give loans to those wishing to build businesses and buy homes in impoverished and minority communities) in mind when they think of illegal structures. However, individualism itself is a structure: it structures the way we think and behave socially. Ideas, patterns of behaviors, and sets of expectations also structure reality.[25] And individualism and consumerism can function as immoral structures: they can reinforce race and class divisions.

25. Helpful insights may be gained here by considering Anthony Giddens's work on "structuration," in which he discusses social mores, behaviors, and social expectations in structural terms; see Giddens, *The Constitution of Society: Outline of the Theory of Structuration* (Berkeley: University of California Press, reprint ed., 1986).

One finds a biblical precursor to this ideological and behavioral structural problem in the New Testament. Gordon Fee says that the sociological divisions between the haves and have-nots in the church in Corinth surfaced in the Lord's Supper, which was likely part of a common meal. It was "sociologically natural for the host to invite those of his/her own class to eat" in the dining room while others ate in the courtyard.[26] "For those who think of themselves as 'keeping the traditions' the actions noted here probably did not register as of particular consequence. They had always acted thus. Birth and circumstances had cast their lots; society had dictated their mores." For Paul, on the other hand, "[t]hose mores at the Lord's Supper were a destruction of the meaning of the Supper itself because it destroyed the very unity which that meal proclaimed" (Fee, p. 544).

The eleventh chapter of 1 Corinthians (v. 22) indicates that the emphatic position of the pronoun "each of you" (*'ekastos*) "highlights the individualistic (i.e., noncommunal) character of the behavior of the rich as they consumed their own meals, in contrast to Paul's emphasis that they are eating *together as the church*" (Fee, p. 541). Paul rebukes them for abusing the church, the Lord's Supper, and Christ himself (Fee, pp. 532-33, 544). The consuming of quantitatively more and qualitatively better food by the haves was a form of autonomy from Christ rather than a sharing in him and in the meal with the whole church. And as such, the haves lost out as well, and that autonomy was consuming the church, distorting and reducing its quality of life. As Fee says, "No 'church' can long endure as the people of God for the new age in which the old distinctions between bond and free (or Jew and Greek, or male and female [or black and white, rich and poor]) are allowed to persist. Especially so at the Table, where Christ, who has made us one, has or-

26. Gordon D. Fee, *The First Epistle to the Corinthians*, The New International Commentary on the New Testament, vol. 7 (Grand Rapids: Eerdmans, 1987), pp. 533-34 [hereafter page references in parentheses in text]; see also Craig Blomberg's discussion of Paul's vision for the church in the Corinthian correspondence and its bearing on homogeneous groupings in certain sectors of the church-growth movement: Craig L. Blomberg, *1 Corinthians*, The NIV Application Commentary (Grand Rapids: Zondervan Publishing Company, 1995), p. 239.

dained that we should visibly proclaim that unity" (p. 544; bracketed material added).

The church too often proclaims disunity as a result of buying into individualistic and commodified consumer versions of spirituality; but, as we can see in the case of Corinth, God will not allow himself or his church to be commodified. The triune, interpersonal God calls people to himself to be ends in themselves, consumed by his holy love as his community, not base commodities consuming one another and being consumed in fiery lust. God's love is expansive, not constricting and reductionist. God's consuming love is creative and expansive, unlike that of the Corinthians; it brings life out of death and breaks down divisions between the haves and the have-nots. Unfortunately, our social settings dictate to us that such love is less valuable, when in actual fact it is more valuable — far more valuable.

Patterns of ideas and behaviors that are enforced and reinforced in our social settings influence the way churches and individuals in churches think and behave, even consume. Commenting on Thorstein Veblen's *The Theory of the Leisure Class,* Bigelow says: "Patterns of consumption and work broadly conform to the boundaries set by class and culture. . . . Veblen saw that it was impossible to understand individual economic choices without understanding the world in which those choices were made."[27] The wealthy Corinthian Christians' habit of eating a lot of good food among themselves and not sharing it with the have-nots followed the patterns of consumption and the boundaries set by their own class and culture. They probably had no idea that their social mores were wrong. They were likely unknowing and insensitive individuals who had been shaped by their culture and who reinforced on a regular basis those patterns of behavior that were already ingrained in them — that is, until Paul rebuked them in view of Christ's kingdom culture. Once exposed, the way they responded would show whether their hearts were with God or with mammon.

The individualistic orientation of evangelicalism structures the church and makes us blind to negative patterns of consumption and sus-

27. Bigelow, "Let There Be Markets: The Evangelical Roots of Economics," p. 38.

picious of structural engagement. Such a suspicion of structural engagement has been present throughout the fundamentalist-evangelical movement's history of contending with and eventually abandoning the denominational structures of mainline Protestantism. Because the evangelical movement abandoned those structures for independence and freedom, it is very difficult for us in the evangelical community today to perceive that we ourselves inhabit structures.

SMALL-GROUP BREEDING GROUND   Not only does evangelicalism's individual-relational-antistructural tendency form us; we are also formed by the homogeneous small-group orientation that has arisen from this framework. Homogeneous, small-group breeding grounds nurture small-minded and shortsighted attempts to address race and class divisions. While helping us become sensitive to one another's struggles with the individualism that is so prominent today,[28] homogeneous small groups desensitize us to the plight of those individuals who are outside our social networks. J. I. Packer says this:

> Evangelical Christianity starts with the individual person: the Lord gets hold of the individual; the individual comes to appreciate certain circles — the smaller circle of the small group, the larger circle of the congregation. These circles are where the person is nurtured and fed and expanded as a Christian. So, we evangelicals are conditioned to think of social structures in terms of what they do for us as individuals. That's all right, but it does lead us to settle too soon for certain self-serving social structures. And we are slow to pick up the fact that some of the social units that we appreciate for that reason can have unhappy spinoff effects on other groups.[29]

28. Robert Wuthnow speaks of the role small groups play in helping people cope with problems associated with individualism and instability so prevalent in society today: Wuthnow, *Sharing the Journey: Support Groups and the Quest for a New Community* (New York: The Free Press, 1996), pp. 317-66.

29. J. I. Packer, quoted in "We Can Overcome," *Christianity Today*, Oct. 2, 2000, p. 43.

Emerson and Smith claim that the very things that drive the white evangelical movement and make it thrive are the things that create obstacles to the attempts to overcome racialization. They go so far as to claim that "white Evangelicalism likely does more to perpetuate the racialized society than to reduce it" (E-S, p. 170). For example, given the vitality of the white evangelical church in America, most congregants spend a large percentage of their time associating with those within their church networks. As a result, their social connections are composed, largely if not exclusively, of people from their own subcultures, blocking meaningful exposure to other groups, including those in the African-American community. It is nearly impossible for those in this boat to see how deep-seated racialization is (E-S, pp. 125-27, 132-33).

When we are not exposed to other groups, we tend to think that frustrated minorities simply have chips on their shoulders, that they are making things up, or that they are exaggerating their difficulties. When middle- and upper-middle-class whites are not exposed to other groups, it is very difficult for them to appreciate the pathos and pain in the following statements: "A piece of property has no value until a white person owns it," or "When will a black woman's blood be seen as being of the same value as a white man's?" The first statement is from a discussion I had with a leading African-American businesswoman and community developer who was lamenting the largely white "pioneer" takeover of northeast Portland right before her eyes.[30] (According to one Portland-area friend of mine, a professor of urban studies, black people in Portland often translate "urban renewal" to mean "negro-removal.") The second statement above was the response of a leading African-American pastor to the events in Portland surrounding the fatal shooting of Kendra James by a white police officer during the summer of 2003.

A lack of exposure to the plight of African-American people has led evangelicals in my social network to say, on numerous occasions, "Look

30. For a detailed analysis of the particular experience of African-Americans in the city of Portland, see *The History of Portland's African American Community — 1805 to the Present* (Portland: Portland Bureau of Planning, 1993).

at the Chinese. They got over it. Why can't the blacks?" What this perspective fails to see is that the scenario is entirely different in scope. Oppression of black people is more severe and culturally ingrained: from being uprooted from their African homeland, to being sold into slavery, torn from their families, denied human rights by government policy, demeaned pervasively by social practices — on and on it goes. The only other ethnic group of people who have faced similar oppression at the hands of Euro-Americans in this country are the Native Americans. And it is heartbreaking to see how *they* have — or have not — survived.[31]

Homogeneous churches and care groups can easily — even though inadvertently — promote and preserve middle-class conservative values. Confronting race and class divisions lacks importance when this value and motivation is present implicitly or explicitly; and confronting the problems becomes counterproductive to the main goal of catering to a middle- or upper-middle-class target audience for Christ. Those targeted would quickly lose interest in Christ and that particular church if it were to suddenly gain interest in addressing these issues. However, while the church may gain that group in the short term, it may be found guilty of blaspheming God's name among the gentiles in the long term, as one lay leader said of his own successful church's homogeneous ways when awakened to these issues.

The long-term possibility that small groups may end up replacing Sunday morning church gatherings, a point made by Robert Wuthnow, is especially unsettling.[32] One community that uses small-group dynamics is the emergent-church movement. The movement is made up of loosely connected, small, and mostly evangelical groups. The movement serves as a radical alternative to the megachurch phenomenon, as well as to traditional church models. Robert Webber compares the emergent church's flowering to the rise of fundamentalism in the twentieth century. Like

---

31. See the following works for treatments of the exploitation of Native-American people: George E. Tinker, *Missionary Conquest: The Gospel and Native American Cultural Genocide* (Minneapolis: Fortress Press, 2003); Vine Deloria, Jr., *Custer Died for Your Sins: An Indian Manifesto* [with a new preface by the author] (Norman, OK: University of Oklahoma Press, 2003).

32. Wuthnow, *Sharing the Journey*, pp. 317-66.

fundamentalism, which was nurtured in tiny community churches, "lots of people are starting neighborhood groups or house churches. The emerging church is being birthed underground. Give it a few years, and it's going to explode."[33] Like fundamentalism was last century, the emergent church will be a cultural force to reckon with in this century.

For all the vitality of small groups and emergent-church gatherings, what will these churches do to help overcome the barriers I have been highlighting in this book? Despite the emergent churches' particular commitments, including a vital concern for the poor and for inter-generational and multicultural dynamics, is there not a real though un-intentional possibility that such churches will further erode the fabric of civil society? Might they not, like fundamentalism, foster another means of departure from multicultural and class inclusion and integration? Why should we raise these questions? Because both small-group and emergent-church arrangements are often based on a preference for af-finity groups.

If a person were to choose a group based on its concern for address-ing poverty and the needs of other racial groups, it is very likely that she would seek out like-minded middle-class or even upwardly mobile Chris-tians like herself who would minister *to* the poor rather than minister *with* the poor as fellow participants of the same group. The latter option is too costly for many, for it involves giving up a certain privileged position as well as sharing ownership with the poor in tackling the problem of pov-erty. Not only does the latter option prove too costly in terms of position; it also proves too costly in terms of the precious commodity of time: it takes too much time and thus is not instrumentally efficient. Such wrongful concerns reveal that a more communal orientation involving sensitivity and solidarity is desperately needed. We must put forth inten-sive efforts toward an intentional inclusion of people from various socio-economic subcultures, or the negative patterning will continue.

33. Robert E. Webber, quoted in John Leland, "Hip New Churches Sway to a Dif-ferent Drummer," *New York Times*, Feb. 18, 2004, section A, p. 1; see also Webber, *The Younger Evangelicals: Facing the Challenges of the New World* (Grand Rapids: Baker Book House, 2002).

While we evangelicals should guard our strengths, we should critically engage our weaknesses. We should address structural evil as we recognize that individualism structures us negatively and often fosters the negative outcomes of homogeneous small groups. While I see the need for some homogeneous groups, such as Alcoholics Anonymous, given the shared need for confidentiality and sensitivity to members' individual addictions, we need to be intentional about creating diversity groups that include members from different ethnic and economic subcultures in order to nurture sensitivity and build understanding and reconciliation among these groups. Lastly, we should address our own consumerist impulses. Rather than quickly leaving our consumer-oriented, homogeneous churches — thus becoming connoisseur Christians ourselves — we should do everything we can, working patiently and lovingly to become transforming agents, helping our own churches transform themselves from the inside out.

One last reason evangelicals have a hard time seeing these things and taking them to heart is the long-standing suspicion in many evangelical quarters of social involvement (as I have noted in the last chapter). But the gospel is social, and we must exhort the church to live out now what will one day be true in all creation, which is how Paul exhorted the Corinthians: he told them to restructure their socioeconomic arrangements in view of God's restructuring of human society through Christ's reconciling work, to which the Lord's Supper bears witness. The gospel promise offers energizing hope that mobilizes the church to participate in God's eschatological future, which has already dawned in Christ's mighty acts on our behalf in history. We need to open our eyes to the triune God's multifaceted kingdom work in our midst, which will expand the homogeneous small group's vision so that it becomes the fellowship of the King.

Expanding the Small Group
to Become the Fellowship of the King

The burden of Frodo and his companions for their beloved community ran deep. Their social solidarity went beyond the bounds of their hobbit, elf, dwarf, wizard, and human identities and affinities — and beyond the identity of their small group. Their confidence in one another more than compensated for their fear of the overwhelming forces arrayed against them. Their defenses and strategies of attack were multifaceted. And they were consumed with the vision of something far greater than Mordor, which helped them withstand evil and conquer it.

We evangelicals have been structured historically and culturally in such a way that we are often blind to the divisive forces arrayed against us. The Bible sheds light on our historical and contemporary situation and provides clues for engagement in the present hour. The remainder of this book provides a biblical and theological paradigm that will illuminate our path and assist us in reordering or restructuring our values, worldview, and practices so that we can conquer and consume the consumer Balrog.

The church must rediscover its own story and its sacramental means of sustenance in order to reconfigure the structures to defeat consumerism and its depersonalization and dehumanization of the world with all that that entails for race and class divisions. Only when the church makes such rediscoveries and reconfigurations will its own witness to the gospel prevail in the struggle against this Balrog and the forces of Mordor. As in the case of Frodo and his friends, it will require that the fellowship be centered in a firm hope in the reigning and returning King.

CHAPTER THREE

Reordering the Cosmic Powers: Turning the Tables at the Stone Table

Delving into the Deeper Magic: Overturning the Fallen Powers

The "magic" of Christ's saving work runs very deep — deeper than any one atonement model can delve.[1] Christ's atoning work cancels out individual sins in addition to defeating the fallen principalities and powers in order to build beloved community. Jesus has provided the necessary condition for living authentically in community. This chapter investigates the deep magic of Christ's atoning work, which serves as the foundation stone for breaking down divisions between God and us and between us and others — including consumer divisions between different races and classes — and making us all one.

In *The Lion, the Witch and the Wardrobe,* the Witch is consumed with adherence to the magic inscribed on the stone table and demands the death of the traitor Edmund. She is a fallen power who is obsessed with the legal code of ransom and justice. In the words of Mr. Beaver, she functions as "the Emperor's hangman." The Witch tells Aslan: "You at least know the magic which the Emperor put into Narnia at the very be-

---

1. Evangelical New Testament scholar and theologian Leon Morris has claimed that all the standard models of the atonement (not just penal substitution) have biblical warrant; there is no such thing as *the* atonement model. Leon Morris, "Atonement, Theories of the," in Walter A. Elwell, ed., *Evangelical Dictionary of Theology* (Grand Rapids: Baker Book House, 1984), pp. 100-102.

ginning. You know that every traitor belongs to me as my lawful prey and that for every treachery I have a right to a kill."[2]

Aslan offers himself in place of Edmund as the flesh for her to consume. Delighted with the exchange, the Witch lets go of Edmund and sinks her teeth into this larger prey. She does not realize that there is a deeper magic inscribed in the stone table:

> [T]hough the Witch knew the Deep Magic, there is a magic deeper still which she did not know. Her knowledge goes back only to the dawn of Time. But if she could have looked a little further back, into the stillness and the darkness before Time dawned, she would have read there a different incantation. She would have known that when a willing victim who had committed no treachery was killed in a traitor's stead, the Table would crack and Death itself would start working backwards.[3]

The Witch and her minions would not have killed the innocent victim, Aslan, if she had known this deeper magic.

This discussion is reminiscent of Paul's words to the Corinthians: "No, we declare God's wisdom, a mystery that has been hidden and that God destined for our glory before time began. None of the rulers of this age understood it, for if they had, they would not have crucified the Lord of glory" (1 Cor. 2:7-8, TNIV). Lewis's account bears witness to Christ's atoning work. It is important to delve into the deeper magic of Christ's atoning work in order to grasp more profoundly what he has done for us in turning the tables on Satan and the other fallen powers and breaking down the walls of division so that all the sons of Adam and daughters of Eve can live together and become one.

Colossians 2:15 shows Christ conquering the fallen powers while on the cross. According to the New Testament, the powers include angelic beings, institutions, and ideas or systems of thought. All three entities influence and structure the way people live. Revelation 2 and 3 reveal

---

2. C. S. Lewis, *The Lion, the Witch and the Wardrobe: A Story for Children* (New York: Macmillan Publishing Company, 1950), pp. 138-39.

3. Lewis, *The Lion, the Witch and the Wardrobe*, pp. 159-60.

that Christ controls the angels (the stars); these angels, in turn, are responsible for the various churches (lampstands). The triune God has authority over the angelic messengers, who oversee the churches (which are *institutions*) and their doctrines, or *ideas* (e.g., the Ephesian church's opposition to false apostles and the Nicolaitans' practices [Rev. 2:2, 6]). Christ defeats the fallen angelic powers (Col. 2:13-23), which are behind the institution that is responsible for promoting the false teaching (or idea) of legalism in the Colossian church.

When rightly related to God, the Creator of all things, those powers are good; but when they seek autonomy from God, they become distorted and reductionist. Such autonomy distorts the ordered and holistic communal dynamics of a true relationship with the Creator and the creation that God intends for all to experience. In the current consumerist cultural context, this often leads to the individualization and commodification of life. Separation from God leads to various forms of separation in the creaturely sphere. When angelic beings, institutions, and ideas become autonomous, they become fallen powers — "Balrogs." The fallen principalities and powers are demonic spirits with personalities and human creations, including social structures, ideas, and perhaps a combination of them all.[4]

Those powers come in many forms, including the Roman Empire and its rule of retribution, pharisaical religion and its legalistic distortion of Israel's election, and the American enterprise and its demands for individual self-fulfillment and consumer preference. Jesus confronts and conquers the powers and the laws by which they wield power: he refuses to play by their rules and masters them rather than being mastered by

4. See the following discussions: J. S. Stewart, "On a Neglected Emphasis in New Testament Theology," *Scottish Journal of Theology* 4 (1951): 292-301; Paul Louis Metzger, "The Sorcerer's Apprentice and the Savior of the World: Space, Time, and Structural Evil," *Cultural Encounters: A Journal for the Theology of Culture* 1, no. 1 (Winter 2004): 85-93; F. F. Bruce and E. K. Simpson, *Commentary on the Epistles to the Ephesians and the Colossians*, The New International Commentary on the New Testament, vol. 10 (Grand Rapids: Eerdmans, 1957), pp. 241-42; Thomas R. Yoder Neufeld, "'Put on the Armour of God': The Divine Warrior from Isaiah to Ephesians," in *Journal for the Study of the New Testament Supplement Series* 140 (London: Sheffield Academic Press, 1997), pp. 122-124.

them. These fallen powers have lost their enslaving grip on people because of the new world order that Jesus has inaugurated in his death and resurrection. As a result, these powers can no longer presume that the enmity they have wedged between various peoples will remain intact.

Jesus has died to his "right" for revenge and retribution on his enemies. Moreover, he has died to his "right" to lordship over the Jewish law and what that would entail for his elevation above all peoples, including his own. And lastly, he has died to his "right" as God Almighty to get what he wants, when he wants it, at the least perceived cost to himself. By dying to these "rights" and rising again in righteousness, Jesus has transcended and transformed the powers. As a result, the powers can now become those whose rule is aimed at serving others, not suppressing them; being guardians of the law for distinguishing peoples, not dividing them; and giving preferential treatment to dispossessed others, not consuming them.

This chapter will center on how Jesus turns the tables on the fallen principalities and powers, beginning with his confronting of Roman rule, will move on to his engagement of the Jewish law, and will close with his attack on the demands of consumerism. The church must bear witness to Jesus and die to its rights if it is to triumph over the powers of the present day.

Overriding the Roman Rule of Retribution

The Witch and her henchmen of C. S. Lewis's fable extend their empire by retribution and suppression. They are unwitting enemies of the Emperor's deeper magic (law) by demanding retributive adherence to it. Their greedy desire for retribution consumes them, even as Aslan consumes their demonic distortion of the Emperor's law, turning the tables on them at the stone table. Aslan eliminates revenge-based justice, with its suppression of and separation of people, by dying in the place of the traitor Edmund, thereby cracking the table in two to make Edmund one with his brother and sisters once again.

The same holds true for Jesus. He confronted the Roman powers by refusing to play by their rules of getting vengeance on enemies by taking matters into their own hands; by refusing to follow that rule, he was not mastered by them.[5] Instead, he entrusted his life to the Father, who loved him; he loved others in return, even asking the Father to forgive those who meant to do him harm (Luke 23:34). While "evil propagates itself by a chain reaction," Jesus brought an end to the vicious cycle of evil propagated through retaliation by absorbing it, taking it upon himself on the cross, entrusting himself to the Father, and thus refusing to retaliate. According to G. B. Caird, "evil is defeated only if the injured person absorbs the evil and refuses to allow it to go any further."[6] Thus Jesus turned the tables on Satan by dying to himself as well as to evil rather than retaliating for the innumerable injustices and insults he bore in his humble incarnate state. Unable to trick Jesus, Satan pushed his plan to the bitter end — and to his own demise — for he unjustly used the righteous law to put the righteous Jesus to death. Because Jesus died to his right to revenge and retribution, the fallen powers have lost their enslaving grip on people and can no longer preserve the enmity or walls of division between them. Jesus has made it possible for all of God's people to be one.

As the righteous one, Jesus has entrusted all judgment to God; hence God has found him worthy to take the book and break its seals. For, unlike the Roman powers that extended their empire by suppression, Jesus has extended the Father's kingdom by purchasing people from every tribe, tongue, people, and nation through his sacrificial death and resurrection (Rev. 5:9). And through his death and resurrection, Jesus has transcended and transformed the powers so that they can now become those whose rule is aimed at serving others, not suppressing them, at bringing unity out of division.

The claim that Jesus was raised, is ascended, and will return challenges current powers that would execute vengeance on their enemies. This transformation of the powers, however, does not seem to be on the

---

5. See Jürgen Moltmann, *The Crucified God: The Cross of Christ as the Foundation and Criticism of Christian Theology* (Minneapolis: Fortress Press, 1993), pp. 136-45, for his distinct treatment of Christ's confrontation of the Roman rule of retribution.

6. G. B. Caird, *Principalities and Powers: A Study in Pauline Theology* (Oxford: Oxford University Press, 1956; reprint, with a foreword by L. D. Hurst, Eugene: Wipf and Stock, 2003), p. 98.

radar screen of some self-identifying leaders of the Moral Majority: they wish to underwrite American democracy in its present form for their own special-interest group by taking back America, while at the same time they are producing apocalyptic thrillers on the holy remnant, the rapture, and the raging beast. Instead of seeking to build and extend beloved community in this world and at this time — in view of that eschatological banquet — they seek to take back America from their enemies, forgetting that judgment belongs to the Lord.

The power-politics religion of all-consuming revenge and retribution symbolized by the Witch and the Roman system is alive and well today. Like Pilate, Herod, and the high priests, the Religious Right and the Left often use Jesus to seek political one-upmanship of power to debase each other. Unlike Jesus — or Martin Luther King, Jr., with his vision of beloved community — many on the Right and the Left seem more concerned with winning rights for their own kinds of people than they are with reconciling all peoples.

Devouring Legalistic Distortions and Divisions

Like Aslan, Christ has devoured the demonic distortion of the law with its ensuing divisions between peoples in order to make us all one. It is not the law that is evil or demonic; rather, it is the impersonal and legalistic use and distortion of the law by the demons. Though nonhuman creation and human structures, including the law, cannot sin, they are part of a fallen cosmos, intertwined inseparably with humanity, which *is* fallen and sinful, and thus those structures are also awaiting redemption.[7]

Scripture and tradition teach that angels were the guardians and messengers of the law (see Gal. 3:19; Heb. 2:2; Jubilees 1:27). In the hands of fallen angels, the law became an oppressive tool for spurring on sin and death rather than an aid to righteous living. The demons held the

---

7. On Caird's reading of the Apostle Paul, the law "becomes demonic" when it "is isolated" from God's grace "and exalted into an independent system of religion. . . . This corruption of the law is the work of sin, and in particular the sin of self-righteousness" (p. 41).

law over the heads of both Jews and gentiles: it was a standard of righteousness they had to attain to be saved.[8] These fallen powers are legalists who are consumed with false adherence to the law. For example, their legalistic account of salvation involved the Judaizing claim that gentiles needed to be circumcised in order to be justified, which created a wall of division between the two groups. I should clarify this: it is not legalistic to speak of Israel's ongoing election or their distinction from the gentiles, who, like them, are saved by faith. Romans 1:16 makes a distinction between these two groups while it still shows them to be peers as the one people of God through their mutual faith in Christ. But it *is* legalistic to argue that there is a division between them, and that the Jewish people, namely, those who are circumcised, are more righteous and more truly God's people than the gentile saints.

The triune God has removed the legalistic separation between them based on a demonic distortion of Israel's election in the law and the enmity that it produces. Ephesians 2:11-21 claims that the triune God has removed divisions between Israel and the nations and has changed gentile strangers and aliens into citizens and members of God's household. God has removed the wall of separation and hostility and has made these peoples one in Christ by the Spirit. Christ has abolished the legalistic divide that separated Jews and gentiles by dying to the law, being unjustly hung on the cursed tree as a righteous man (Gal. 3:13-14). On the cross, Jesus took upon himself the hostility that Jews and gentiles demonstrated toward one another and conquered the demonic forces that sowed such division and enmity (Eph. 2:14-15; Col. 2:13-15). Caird's comments are instructive:

> By drawing off on to himself the hostility with which men regarded one another, and by allowing it to put him on the Cross, he has slain the hostility. But it should be noted that the hostility between Pharisee and sinner and between Jew and Gentile was an inevitable consequence of the tyranny of the law. The slaying of the hostility involved

8. See Bruce and Simpson, *Ephesians and Colossians,* pp. 239-42, for Bruce's discussion of Col. 2:15; see also Caird, *Principalities and Powers,* pp. 48-49, for the latter's treatment of Jewish and gentile "enslavement" to the demonic rule involving the perversion of law.

the abolition of the law, and so constituted a victory over the angelic guardians of legal religion.[9]

Satan no doubt thought he could do away with Jesus' efforts of atoning for sin, either by tricking him into asserting his rights over the law and by refusing to face judgment on behalf of fallen humanity or by binding him to death forever. Satan's distortion of the law in the depiction of Jesus' temptation in Matthew 4 (which is bound up with his atoning work) served the former tactic, but to no avail. For Jesus, unlike other people, could "absorb all that the powers could do to him and . . . neutralize it by his unwavering obedience to God."[10] Jesus refused to assert his lordship as the Son of God over the law; instead, he put himself under the law as the Son of Man in obedience to the Father and in identification with fallen humanity. And so, in placing himself under the law (as initiated in Matt. 4), Jesus triumphed over the Devil and thus climbed the mount (Matt. 5) not to get the law but to give it anew — the law of grace administered not by angels but through him (see the Sermon on the Mount [Matt. 5–7]; cf. Heb. 1–3). He placed himself under the law to redeem those enslaved under the death-bringing law in order that they might live anew as God's sons and daughters by the law of the Spirit of life, the Spirit of Christ who dwells in them (Gal. 4:4-7; Rom. 8:1-2).

Jesus undermined the legalistic law-breaking of the principalities and powers through his keeping of the law, and thus he was raised from the dead to new life through the same Spirit who now raises us, giving us new life (1 Pet. 3:18; Rom. 8:8-11; Gal. 4:4-6). Not only did Jesus bring an end to the legalistic use of the law; he brought an end to sin and death as well. And he brought about in their wake a new beginning to the created order, freeing people from the demonic spell (Rom. 8:1-4; Gal. 4:1-7). Thinking that they had tabled Jesus through his judgment unto death, the powers found, to their utter horror, that in undergoing judgment he judged them, thereby turning the tables on them and freeing humanity

9. Caird, *Principalities and Powers*, p. 99. I do not wish to imply that the law is abolished, but that it is reinterpreted in light of grace to include gentiles as equal participants with Israel in Christ apart from circumcision of the flesh.

10. Caird, *Principalities and Powers*, p. 98.

— Jews and gentiles — from its oppressors (1 Cor. 2:6-10; Eph. 2:14-15; Col. 2:13-15).

The preceding account is a classic case of turning the tables on the principalities and powers, making it possible for Paul to say in Colossians 2:13-15:

> When you were dead in your sins and in the uncircumcision of your sinful nature, God made you alive with Christ. He forgave us all our sins, having canceled the written code, with its regulations, that was against us and that stood opposed to us; he took it away, nailing it to the cross. And having disarmed the powers and authorities, he made a public spectacle of them, triumphing over them by the cross.[11]

Like Aslan, who turned the tables on the White Witch and her forces by offering himself to be sacrificed on the stone table, Christ turned the tables on the principalities and powers by veiling himself in creaturely flesh and humbling himself to death on the cross. To their horror, the cross — in view of his resurrection (Col. 2:11; 1 Pet. 3:22) — has become the throne from which he reigns and the weapon by which he has demolished the wall of separation and enmity that they had erected between the Jews and gentiles. As the Lord over the law, Jesus has died to his "right" to lordship over the Hebrew law and what that would entail for his elevation above all peoples, including his own. By rising again, Jesus has transcended and transformed the powers so that they can become what they were in-

---

11. Colin Gunton says that Wesley Carr makes a conceivable case that the powers in Colossians 2:15 refer to the heavenly host serving as Christ's cheering section rather than to Christ's enemies. Nonetheless, Gunton argues that, regardless of its meaning in Colossians 2:15, the NT presents Jesus as victorious in battle over forces that enslave humanity. Gunton, *The Actuality of Atonement: A Study of Metaphor, Rationality, and the Christian Tradition* (Edinburgh: T&T Clark, 1989), pp. 55-57; see also Wesley Carr, *Angels and Principalities: The Background, Meaning and Development of the Pauline Phrase "hai archai kai hai exousiai"* (Cambridge, UK: Cambridge University Press, 2005), pp. 168-71, 176. Perhaps there is something to be said for the opinions of someone like Caird and Carr, namely, that the conquered and vanquished foes, those angelic powers, submit to Christ (see Caird, *Principalities and Powers*, p. 99), thus becoming his cheering section on his triumphant march.

tended to be as created (see Col. 1:16), that is, guardians of the law rightly administered for distinguishing peoples, not dividing them.

It is not the *distinction* between Jews and gentiles that is demonic, but rather the *division* between them (recall the rightful distinction between Jews and gentiles as discussed above). The divinely appointed distinction between them is found in Matthew 10:5 and Romans 1:16; the demonically inspired division between them is found in Acts 15:1. We must also speak here of the demonic and arrogant antagonism to the law among the gentile Christians, which involved the claim that Israel's election has been superseded in favor of the inclusion of the gentiles in God's covenantal purposes by faith (Rom. 11:11-24). Separation (legalism) as well as supersessionism (gentile Christians displacing Israel) and antinomianism (antagonism to the law) are all equally demonic.

While it is important to guard against reading into the New Testament an American segregationist-integrationist perspective on race,[12] the New Testament's focus on how God in Christ reconciles alienated social groups (such as Israel and the nations[13]) does shed light on present-day conflicts between peoples, including racial and economic tensions. Just as Jewish Christians failed to grasp the radical nature of Christ's embrace of the gentiles as equal-though-distinct participants in the one people of God when they required those gentile believers to be

---

12. In a very helpful pamphlet, Richard Soulen says: "The motivation of Israel's ethnocentrism was . . . not racial in nature. *It was ethnic and at heart religious.*" Richard N. Soulen, *Race and Biblical Faith* [with a study guide by Carole Vaughn] (Richmond, VA: Division of Political & Human Rights Board of Church & Society, Virginia Annual Conference, United Methodist Church, 1984), p. 16; see also p. 7 for a discussion of the origins of understanding race in physical terms. See also Dave Unander's work, *Shattering the Myth of Race: Genetic Realities and Biblical Truth* [foreword by John M. Perkins] (Valley Forge, PA: Judson Press, 2000).

13. For a reading of Romans that takes seriously "Jew" and "gentile" as significant religious and ethnic categories in Paul's thought, see Stanley K. Stowers, *A Rereading of Romans: Justice, Jews, and Gentiles* (New Haven: Yale University Press, 1994); see esp. the discussion on p. 34. Regarding Israel and the nations and the social and corporate dimensions of Paul's thought, see the following works by Markus Barth: *The Broken Wall: A Study of the Epistle to the Ephesians* (Philadelphia: Judson Press, 1959); *The People of God* (Sheffield, UK: JSOT Press, 1983).

circumcised and become Jewish in accordance with a legalistic reading of the law, many in the church today have failed to grasp the radical nature of Christ's embrace when they have unwittingly promoted or supported divisions between people based on slave laws, Jim Crow laws, and the free-market law of consumer preference. Throughout its history, the church has often failed to grasp the liberating message of the New Testament that Jesus has done away with the dividing wall of hostility between Jew and gentile, male and female, and slave and free (Gal. 3:28).

Jesus, as the liberator, inaugurated the ultimate Year of Jubilee, which involves freedom for all who are imprisoned and oppressed, not simply Israelites (Luke 4:18-19, 23-27). (In the Old Testament, freedom was to be granted only to fellow Israelites in the Year of Jubilee.) Jesus' inauguration of the ultimate Year of Jubilee no doubt led Paul to challenge the ancient system of slavery. While Paul did plant churches in contexts where slavery was practiced, he also viewed this situation against a larger backdrop. Paul saw himself as living between the times, and he saw the church as the eschatological community of the new humanity. Thus Paul challenged the broader society's slave structure, contending against it in the church. He urged Philemon to free Onesimus and to treat him as an equal in the church, which was probably meeting in Philemon's house. Paul also subverted the Roman system of authority and slavery by referring to himself in the Epistle to Philemon as a "prisoner of Christ Jesus" (v. 1), and by referring in Philippians to Timothy and himself as "servants of Christ Jesus" (Phil. 1:1). Paul even challenged the Roman hierarchy by telling masters to treat their slaves with respect because they served a common master who is no respecter of persons (Eph. 6:9; cf. Col. 3:25–4:1). Elsewhere, Paul encouraged slaves to gain their freedom if they could (1 Cor. 7:21), and he called the believing slave "the Lord's freedman" and the believing free man "Christ's slave" (1 Cor. 7:22).

Paul's exhortations and admonitions certainly bore implications for the abolitionist debate in the nineteenth century. However, the church's confronting of the powers — with calls for breaking down the walls of division between Jews and gentiles, masters and slaves, and whites and blacks — must not end in the nineteenth or twentieth centuries. And, in view of Christ's saving work, the church must also call for breaking down the walls of division based on the law of consumer preference, which enslaves supposedly free people today.

Dying to the Law of Consumerism and Rising to New Life

Self-satisfying greed for Turkish Delight fed Edmund's disregard for his own brother and sisters in *The Lion, the Witch and the Wardrobe*. As a result, he fell prey to the White Witch's own calculating greed. Yet the Witch failed to see how Aslan turned the tables on such greedy calculus at the stone table, for he knew of a far deeper, liberating magic than what the law of consumer preference, with its consumption of Turkish Delight, had to offer.

The demonic division in Jesus' and Paul's day between the Jewish and gentile peoples was religious, not racist; it was bound up with a legalistic interpretation of the law and Israel's *election* espoused by some members of the Jewish community, on the one side, and the supersessionist orientation espoused by some of the gentile Christians, on the other. Today the American church's division between groups of people involving ethnicities, classes, and the like is also often religious, even legalistic, though not in the same way. Rather, it is a legalistic division based on consumer *selection:* people have the God-given right to choose or select what churches they wish to attend based on preference and taste. One might liken it to a libertarian notion of free will. This doctrine of natural (or perhaps, unnatural) selection, the inalienable and God-given freedom to choose freely from among a host of options, is not unique to the church. It is a doctrine held dear by a vast number of Americans — a sign of their enlightenment, of their coming of age, and of their assurance of their own secular salvation.

The dominant structure of the evangelical church today favors, fosters, and shapes its structures around the key ingredient of individual choice — though not always obedience. One will find disordered priorities and unwitting segregationist practices where norms of consumer preference and privatized spirituality exist. It is hardly necessary to have Jim Crow legislation. James was no doubt reflecting his disgust about the church's preferential treatment of the rich and its neglect of widows and orphans in their distress (James 1:27–2:7) when he wrote the following words to the church of his day:

> Who is wise and understanding among you? Let them show it by their good life, by deeds done in the humility that comes from wisdom. But if you harbor bitter envy and selfish ambition in your hearts, do not boast about it or deny the truth. Such "wisdom" does not come down from heaven but is earthly, unspiritual, demonic. For where you have envy and selfish ambition, there you find disorder and every evil practice. (James 3:13-16, TNIV)

Selfish ambition is demonic; it is now, as it was then. It arises from the pit, not from above, and it confuses godly living with living the good life. Just as it did in Edmund's selfish ambition to consume as much Turkish Delight as the Witch could possibly give him — no matter what the cost to his relationships with his siblings (the daughters of Eve and the other son of Adam) — such unwise ambition wittingly or unwittingly leads to social disorder and evil practices. The way churches today cater to the market forces of homogeneity and upward mobility inevitably leads them to exclude from their fellowship the poor and those on the fringes of society, partly because they have made such outsiders feel uncomfortable with the insider crowd of "our kind of people." Dehumanizing freedom of infinite choice and personal preference inside and outside the church replaces the law of enforcement and impersonal rule, and that reinforces the race and class divide. Today's problems of race and class in America are not rooted in torture or oppression, but in liberated choice and pleasure: they are bound up with the subtle law of consumer preference. This law declares that one must choose in order to be real, to be righteous, to be justified, and to be enlightened.

The Bible does not address the problem of consumerism directly, at least not as an ideology; that would be an anachronism. Yet, to the extent that consumerism splits the church, it comes under the prophetic purview mapped out in Scripture's call to holy unity. Church-growth strategies that emphasize quantitative over qualitative enlargement and cater to consumer choice and personal preference whet the appetites of the demonic powers as malevolent consumers and breed disunity. In this light, they warrant Scripture's rebuke. The book of Ephesians places a great deal of emphasis on unity. The discussion of the armor of God and spiritual warfare (Eph. 6) should be read with unity in mind. It has prompted one pastor who is committed to urban reconciliation to write that the principalities and powers

> would want nothing more than to attempt to destroy the "new man" (Eph. 2:15) of which Christ is the head. So Paul reminds us that our real struggle is not against others in the church ("flesh and blood"), but against the powers that *ultimately* lurk behind all relational conflict and have as their intent to hinder the expression of authentic unity. This would certainly apply to the demonic attempt to thwart any authentic manifestation of unity between culture, race, etc., in the local church. For this reason, I am not too excited about the "homogeneous unit" principle. It may provide for rapid numerical growth, but seems to de-emphasize a qualitative growth element that is so vital to our witness as the body of Christ (see John 17).[14]

The church must contend against the fallen powers (including consumerism) that wage war on biblical unity. As Paul points out to the carnal and fleshly Corinthians, had the greedy rulers of this age known the secret wisdom of God, that by dying to himself Christ would consume them, "they would not have crucified the Lord of glory." But they did, and so they are "coming to nothing" (1 Cor. 2:6-8). Tables turned.

Satan's temptation of Jesus (Matt. 4) is a classic table-turning, demonstrating that Christ reigns over the fallen principalities and powers in their particular libertarian tactics of temptation and oppression. As the prince of the demons, Satan is the prime and primal consumer. According to one classic interpretation of Isaiah 14's account of the morning star and Ezekiel 28's account of the King of Tyre (which John Milton likely had in mind in his portrayal of Lucifer's fall in *Paradise Lost*[15]), Luci-

---

14. David Stevens, letter to author, Feb. 25, 2004.

15. Milton, *Paradise Lost*, ed. Christopher Ricks (London: Penguin Books, 1968), pp. 125-31. Caird rejects Milton's view that Satan's fall preceded the creation of the world, al-

fer becomes consumed with his own beauty and covets God's throne. When he falls, he wants to take captive God's human creation. So he baits and switches not only the historical king of Tyre, who sinned violently through his widespread trade, but also this king's predecessors, those primal humans Adam and Eve, who, like the morning star, longed to ascend to the throne of God by consuming what was so tasty and pleasing to the eye and desirable for gaining wisdom. On this reading, Satan darkens human understanding and imprisons the human race by means of his false promises of self-realization and liberation through consumption.On the other hand, the Second Adam is tempted — as all humans are — and yet triumphs in their place and on their behalf. While pagans fall prey to Satan's false promises of enlightenment, self-realization, and mastery through consuming, and are thereby darkened in their understanding and enslaved, Satan falls prey to Christ, who turns the tables on him: Christ does so by denying himself the very things he deserves as God's anointed king. Christ also turns the tables on our ambitions. It is not by choosing and consuming but by being chosen and consumed by Christ that we triumph over Satan. By being chosen and consumed by Christ, we are justified, assured, liberated, and enlightened. Christ has turned the tables to clear space for all of us to sit down and to share freely from the abundant table of his reconciliation. No longer must we remain at Satan's table of ravenous consumption and greedy ambition, where there is always a lot, but never enough to go around.

The devil can never get enough. And though he fails in his temptation of Jesus, that does not prevent him from trying again. Jesus captures and consumes Satan by rising from the dead, for Satan's power is but weakness before the resurrection of the crucified Jesus. Jesus defeats Satan in his life on earth beginning with his temptation and ending with

---

though he acknowledges that it "can be traced back to Jewish sources." Caird, *Principalities and Powers*, p. 31. Here Caird points to Slav. En. xxix. 4 ff. (see Caird, p. 31, note 1). Regardless of the merits of this classic interpretation of the origins of Satan's fall, it is accurate in its assessment of Satan's ongoing activity of seeking to lure humanity away from God — as in the case of the Garden of Eden story and the account of Christ's temptation, which were similar to C. S. Lewis's portrayal of the demons in *The Screwtape Letters*.

his crucifixion. Jesus has now restructured creaturely life through his resurrection. He has died to his "right" as God Almighty to get what he wants in order to give us what we need. By rising again, Jesus has transcended and transformed the powers so that they can now become the driving forces for advancing others' interests, not pursuing personal preferences. This is not simply a matter of his own individual choice, for the whole cosmic order has been turned upside down. Jesus' resurrection reconfigures life and its priorities so that God's people can die to the yuppie dream and live anew to this nobler vision of reality. Although the consumer church is a fallen power, it can be transformed when it is consumed by Jesus so that it may bear witness as a kind of first fruits of Jesus' new world order.

Cleaning House and Cleansing Temples

The atoning work of Christ involves the restructuring of the elemental powers of the universe, to which the church is called to bear witness. The whole creation now awaits the unity of the church, which the torn veil and destroyed wall in the temple prefigure — a unity with God, to be sure, but also with one's fellows. Thus the apostle can write:

> For he himself is our peace, who has made the two one, and has destroyed the barrier, the dividing wall of hostility, by abolishing in his flesh the law with its commandments and regulations. His purpose was to create in himself one new man out of the two, thus making peace, and in this one body to reconcile both of them to God through the cross, by which he put to death their hostility. He came and preached peace to you who were far away and peace to those who were near. For through him we both have access to the Father by one Spirit. Consequently, you are no longer foreigners and aliens, but fellow citizens with God's people and members of God's household, built on the foundation of the apostles and prophets, with Christ Jesus himself as the chief cornerstone. In him the whole building is joined together and rises to become a holy temple in the Lord. And in

83

him you too are being built together to become a dwelling in which God lives by his Spirit. (Eph. 2:14-22)

The Princeton Proposal for Christian Unity draws attention to the fact that the book of Ephesians "presents the whole Christian mystery as the mystery of God's unification of all things in Christ (1:10), which takes form most concretely in the reconciliation of Jew and Gentile 'in one body through the cross' (2:16)." A few sentences later, the statement says: "Ephesians . . . sketches an amazing cosmic vision in which the very meaning and destiny of creation are displayed in the life of small Christian assemblies in which Jew and Gentile struggle to live together with Christ as their peace."[16] Together they make up the temple of God in which God lives by the Spirit (Eph. 2:22).

Christ has reconfigured the structures through his life, death, and resurrection, having been led and empowered by God's Spirit (Luke 4:1, 18), having offered himself up to death through the Spirit without blemish (Heb. 9:14), and having been raised by the Spirit to new life (1 Pet. 3:18). God has, through Christ, torn from top to bottom the veil in the temple that separated people from the divine presence (Matt. 27:51), and God has destroyed the dividing wall of hostility in the temple courts that separated the nations from Israel (Eph. 2:14-16). Now Jews and Gentiles "both have access to the Father by one Spirit" — through Christ (Eph. 2:18). Christ has made them all members of God's household.

This work continues today, but the church must guard against other forces at work today, those forces that seek to rebuild the old structures and walls that divide diverse peoples. Moneychangers and merchants have once again turned God's temple into a market. Jesus cleansed the temple in his day: he scattered the coins and overturned the tables of the moneychangers, and he cast out the merchants from the Court of the Gentiles (Mark 11; John 2). He yelled at them: "Stop turning my Father's house into a market!" (John 2:16, TNIV) and "My

16. Carl E. Braaten and Robert W. Jenson, eds., *In One Body through the Cross: The Princeton Proposal for Christian Unity* (Grand Rapids: Eerdmans, 2003), pp. 30-31.

house will be called a house of prayer for all nations" (Mark 11:17). The temple-cleansing prefigures the unity between all peoples that Pentecost truly inaugurates and the book of Ephesians describes: it incorporates the Jews, God's elect people, and the gentiles into God's household, where Christ seats everyone at the same table.[17]

Jesus needs to cleanse the temple again today; he needs to overturn the tables of commerce and consumption, for consumer Christianity continues to turn the temple into a market. Greedy zeal for a false utopian vision of homogeneity and upward mobility threatens to consume the church, rebuilding the wall of division between those of different ethnicities and classes through free-market consumer church-growth strategies, as well as prosperity-gospel preaching to the poor. Concerning the latter, John Perkins argues:

> The prosperity movement is heavily accepted among the poor but has done very little in terms of real community development at the grassroots level. It takes people's attention away from the real problem, and if those people succeed it encourages them to remove themselves from the very people they ought to be identifying with and working among.[18]

Jesus identifies with the poor, and he challenges us to identify with them as well. In view of this, it is worth pointing out that, while Joel Osteen's megachurch (Lakewood Church in Houston) draws scores of people from diverse ethnic backgrounds due to his positive, prosperity-gospel messages, his "bloom where you're planted" orientation does not appear to be about staying put and identifying with those who do not yet have their "best life now." The prosperity gospel never seems to focus on community development, but on developing and elevating oneself — and not on the cross, like Jesus and Paul (John 12:27-33; Gal. 2:20). Jesus challenges us to have the best lives we can possibly have *now*, as we die to ourselves daily in view of his kingdom, which is *not yet*

---

17. See Caird's discussion of this point in *Principalities and Powers*, pp. 98-99.

18. John M. Perkins, *Beyond Charity: The Call to Christian Community Development* (Grand Rapids: Baker Books, 1993), p. 71.

realized in full (see Matt. 6:19-21; Luke 9:23-25; Luke 12:32-34; John 12:24-26).[19]

This same Jesus who challenges us also comforts us, for our true hope lies not in our political agendas and Laodicean utopias but in the resurrected Lord. Satan, who is the archetype of the fallen powers and the true, iconic projection of our fallen condition, believes he has the right to kill Jesus on the stone table, and his greedy sense of entitlement and his individualistic self-assertion come out in the forms of retribution, legalism, and consumerism. But the solitary, sacrificial Jesus is not truly alone as he lies on the table before the devil and his minions. For as the incarnate Son, who lives by the Spirit of God and offers himself up as a sacrifice, he entrusts himself to the Father to raise him from the dead in order to defeat the powers and create a community that finds life by relinquishing its rights to retributive rule, legalistic exclusion, and consumer preference.

The Christian religion is not an opiate of the masses; rather, it offers energizing hope that mobilizes the church to become downwardly mobile and to partner with the downtrodden to take action and do something about their oppressive circumstances. The church is to live in the present in light of God's future, which has already dawned in Christ's mighty act on its behalf in history. Christ's atoning and transforming work in the Spirit creates hope not only for the future but for life in the present as well. The triune God has set in motion a conversion to a new world order that ultimately involves the conversion of the individual and the conversion of church polity configurations. The table-turning at the stone table on our behalf leads ultimately to the cleansing or restructuring of the individual person as a temple of God (1 Cor. 6:19) and of the

---

19. See the following references to Joel Osteen and his work: "Meet the Prosperity Preacher," May 23, 2005: www.businessweek.com/magazine/content/05_21/b3934014_mzoo1.htm (posted April 5, 2007); Diana Keough, "Interview" with Joel Osteen about his book *Your Best Life Now: 7 Steps to Living at Your Full Potential*, December 15, 2004: www.faithfulreader.com/authors/au-osteen-joel.asp (posted April 6, 2007); Dominique, "Notes from My Church-Word of God Speak, Fall Down Like Rain," April 3, 2007: http://1800gospel.com/2007/04/notes-from-my-church-word-of-god-speak-fall-down-like-rain/ (posted April 6, 2007).

community of people as the ultimate temple of God (1 Cor. 3:16-17). The Holy Spirit, who rearranged Christ's position by raising him from the dead, rearranges hearts and community structures so that they are centered on Christ. The triune God's redemptive advance has provided the necessary conditions for us to triumph, which makes possible the restructuring of our individual lives, church polity configurations, and the church's civic involvement, so that we no longer have to be retreating fortresses, battle camps, and homogeneous units. I have discussed the conversion to the new world order through Christ's atoning work. In the remaining chapters I will address these necessary forms of restructuring, beginning with the supernatural shakeup of individual hearts and lives.

CHAPTER FOUR

Reordering the Christian's Life: The Supernatural Shakeup

Shaking Up the Veg-o-matic Faith

Neo, one of the characters in a recent book, says that the definition of "saved" has been "shrunken and freeze-dried by modernity." Neo calls for

> a postmodern consideration of what salvation means, something beyond an individualized and consumeristic version. I may have a personal home, personal car, personal computer, personal identification number, personal digital assistant, personal hot-tub — all I need now is personal salvation from my own personal savior . . . this all strikes me as Christianity diced through the modern Veg-o-matic. . . .[1]

While I would settle for a biblical over a modern or postmodern view of salvation, I agree with Neo that we have often sliced, diced, and compartmentalized "saved" to the private and personal realm of consumer passions. What is required is a holistic, supernatural shakeup where the slicing and dicing being done is the pruning of the vine's branches recorded in John 15 so that Christ's followers may bear more abundant fruit on that vine, who is Christ. Such a shakeup is from the inside out and will remove from us our individualistic consumer passions; it will

1. Brian D. McLaren, *A New Kind of Christian: A Tale of Two Friends on a Spiritual Journey* (San Francisco: Jossey-Bass, 2001), p. 130.

88

turn us upside down to love holistically, just as God loves. According to the Bible and the best exponents of evangelical theology and practice, the two always go together — and in that order. Together they constitute the supernatural shakeup.

Structural engagement is vitally necessary. But it is not enough. Being "born again" (or from above), in spite of all its negative connotations, is also necessary for overcoming race and class barriers in a consumer church. One must be turned inside out and upside down. The fight against racialization and related problems requires regeneration, repentance, and forgiveness — the key ingredients of being "born again." Emerson and Smith also sense the need for highlighting classical evangelical emphases when they say:

> Evangelicals have some important contributions to offer for the solution to racial division in the United States — such as their stress on the importance of primary relationships, and the need for confession and forgiveness. These may be important because, given the long, tumultuous history of U.S. black-white relations, solutions that call only for structural change are probably as naïve as solutions that merely ask individuals to make some friends across race. The collective wounds over race run deep. They need to be healed. And for healing to take place, there will have to be forgiveness.[2]

Moreover, the evangelical emphasis on personal responsibility is also vitally important. In addition to overturning victimizing structures, people should never make excuses for taking part in victimizing activities and should never play the victim card. Our failure to take responsibility for our actions is very dehumanizing, whether we are acting as victimizer or victim. We are personally responsible for our actions, no matter how much victimizing structures condition us; yet, though we are personally responsible, we are not alone and thus should not abandon hope. We have a personal and powerful Savior who can deliver us from the role of victimizer or victim. Marguerite Shuster speaks to this:

2. Michael O. Emerson and Christian Smith, *Divided by Faith: Evangelical Religion and the Problem of Race in America* (New York: Oxford University Press, 2000), pp. 170-71.

Not, of course, that we should lose sight of the labors and insights of those who have sensitized us to the devastating effects of structural and systemic evils, including oppression and discrimination in their myriad forms. Sin is not just a matter of small-scale personal nastiness. Nor would we deny that genetic and biochemical factors give some people predispositions and vulnerabilities from which others are free. . . . Nonetheless, loss of the category of sin at the individual level more surely robs us of dignity and of hope than does the most punishing "miserable sinner" theology of another age. After all, "miserable sinners" retain the status of those who have responsibility for their behavior and the prospects of a Savior who can deliver them. Those who are only victims of governments, cultures, psychology, or biology are shut up to whatever help compassion for their state may (or may not) evoke, whatever healing a new technology may provide, or whatever transformations the latest public reform efforts or private bootstrap operations may produce — a set of options that should not cheer the clear-eyed observer of human history. These efforts to protest individual innocence, that is, come at an extremely high — not to mention unbiblical — price.[3]

It is important to balance the personal and structural. In fact, we must pay attention to the restructuring of the human heart so that we can personally and corporately take responsibility for confronting and overturning oppressive structures such as homogeneity, upward mobility, and consumerism. In all of this, it is not a matter of deciding to take a Matrix-like red or blue pill (relational and structural in this case) to free ourselves. Maybe take both.

Highlighting evangelical "contributions" will make up the bulk of this chapter: in specific terms, I want to focus on conversion/regeneration as well as reformation. Conversion/regeneration is bound up with reconciliation with God, while reformation is bound up with reconciliation with our fellow humans. We need to pray for a fresh outpouring of the Spirit of revival that will lead to regeneration and reformation if we

3. Marguerite Shuster, *The Fall and Sin: What We Have Become as Sinners* (Grand Rapids: Eerdmans, 2004), p. 101.

are to heal the disease-stricken church. The evangelical community must appropriate these classic evangelical emphases to overcome race and class barriers in the consumer church age.

I will focus on turning the tables on the individual heart; in so doing, I want to counter two extremes: *moralism* on the one hand and *escapism* on the other. I will argue that the love-transformed heart and lifestyle chart a course beyond both. Evangelical urbanologist Ray Bakke has spoken of the need for Christians to cultivate a cruciform Christian existence that accounts for the vertical and horizontal dimensions of reality. The vertical dimension signifies piety, that is, one's relationship with God; the horizontal dimension involves social activism. A neglect of the vertical dimension leads to moralism, while a neglect of the horizontal dimension leads to escapism.[4]

Although it is important to account for both directions of the cruciform existence, it is vital to begin with the vertical. Attempts to confront race and class divisions can be intense and overwhelming and will not bear lasting fruit — indeed, could end in anger or apathy — unless we experience the undying love of God that is poured out into our hearts through the Spirit of grace, whom God in Christ freely gives us to transform our hearts and lives (Rom. 5:5; John 3:1-8; 7:37-39; 15:1-17; 1 Cor. 13). What is required is a great awakening, a turning of the tables of the heart in which the Spirit inspires within us an all-consuming passion to follow the downwardly mobile Christ into the world. Given that such awakenings are entirely dependent on divine initiative, we must address the problem of moralism before going on to escapism.

4. Raymond Bakke made this point while speaking at First Covenant Church, Portland, OR, Feb. 5, 2003; see also his discussion of the need to synthesize the personal spirituality of Philippians and the public spirituality of Colossians in Bakke, *A Theology as Big as the City* (Downers Grove, IL: InterVarsity Press, 1997), pp. 158-62.

Moving Beyond Moralism:
The Love-Transformed Heart

According to a properly framed evangelical ethics, the unilateral relationship between the vertical and horizontal dimensions implies that a converted heart will manifest itself in concern for the neighbor (1 John 4:7-21). But the flipside of that is not equally true: concern for the neighbor does not necessarily flow from a converted heart. Emphasis on divine grace, not human capability, is the central feature of the evangelical ethical perspective. Donald Bloesch speaks of this peculiarly evangelical ethical orientation in his discussion of "Evangelical contextualism," which he associates with Karl Barth, Dietrich Bonhoeffer, and Helmut Thielicke:

> Evangelicals in this tradition speak more of graces than of virtues. Virtues indicate the unfolding of human potentialities, whereas graces are manifestations of the work of the Holy Spirit within us. It is not the fulfillment of human powers but the transformation of the human heart that is the emphasis in an authentically evangelical ethics.[5]

One person whom Bloesch does not specifically mention, yet someone who is centrally located in this ethical tradition, is the father of American evangelicals, Jonathan Edwards (1703-1758). The doctrine of the Spirit plays a central role in Edwards's understanding of the Christian life and ethics, a role that begins with the saints' union with God. Only through such a heart transformation and participation in the triune action of God through Christ and the Spirit does human action bear lasting fruit and find its true fulfillment. I will focus on Edwards because of his central place in America's religious life, including his role as the father of American evangelicalism.[6] As George Marsden says, American

---

5. Donald G. Bloesch, *Freedom for Obedience: Evangelical Ethics in Contemporary Times* (San Francisco: Harper & Row, Publishers, 1987), p. 191.

6. This is the claim of Jay Tolson in "The New Old-Time Religion," *U. S. News and World Report*, Dec. 8, 2003, p. 38. Edwards's relationship to evangelicalism is also discussed in Nathan O. Hatch and Harry S. Stout, eds., *Jonathan Edwards and the American Experience* (New York: Oxford University Press, 1988).

history "recounted without its religious history of Edwards is like *Moby Dick* without the whale."[7]

Above and beyond Edwards's importance for the First Great Awakening, his venerable position in nineteenth-century America, a hundred years after he had died, was also profound. According to Joseph Conforti, Edwards was hailed as an "esteemed cultural icon, father of the Great Awakening and of American revivalism, and embodiment of a lofty standard of evangelical piety. . . ."[8] Conforti says that "the Second Great Awakening also witnessed a kind of 'reinvention' of Edwards as a founding father of evangelical America's emerging benevolent empire of revivalism, piety, and reform."[9] There has recently been a renewed interest in Edwards among Protestant evangelicals due in part to an appropriation of his thought by evangelical leaders such as John Piper.[10]

I will use Edwards's theology and ethical theory in an attempt to move beyond the debased visions of moralism and escapism noted above. It is important at the outset to investigate Edwards's concept of the triune God's union with believers because that bears directly on his ethical model and thus on confronting moralism.[11] For Edwards, the Spirit who

7. George Marsden, quoted in Jay Tolson, "The New Old-Time Religion," p. 38. Two books that chronicle Edwards's significance for American religion and theology are George M. Marsden, *Jonathan Edwards: A Life* (New Haven: Yale University Press, 2003) and Robert W. Jenson, *America's Theologian: A Recommendation of Jonathan Edwards* (New York: Oxford University Press, 1988).

8. Joseph A. Conforti, *Jonathan Edwards, Religious Tradition, and American Culture* (Chapel Hill, NC: The University of North Carolina Press, 1995), p. 56.

9. Conforti, *Jonathan Edwards*, p. 9. Perhaps John R. Mott and the Student Volunteer Movement at the end of the nineteenth and beginning of the twentieth century fits this description, given the movement's aim to bring the gospel and American civil society to the world.

10. See John Piper, *God's Passion for His Glory: Living the Vision of Jonathan Edwards* (Wheaton: Crossway Books, 1998).

11. Two recent works on Edwards have shown the significance of the doctrine of the Trinity for Edwards's intellectual and ethical paradigm: see Amy Plantinga Pauw, *The Supreme Harmony of All: The Trinitarian Theology of Jonathan Edwards* (Grand Rapids: Eerdmans, 2002) and William J. Danaher, Jr., *The Trinitarian Ethics of Jonathan Edwards* (Louisville: Westminster John Knox Press, 2004).

unites Father and Son is the same Spirit who dwells within all believers, uniting them to God. In his "Treatise on Grace," Edwards claims that the indwelling Spirit constitutes believers in an "immediate" manner, ministering as a "vital principle" of God's love in their souls, uniting them to Christ. Christ dwells in each of the saints' hearts through this very Spirit, who is the love of God: "The way in which Christ dwells in the saints is by His Spirit's dwelling in them."[12] In *Religious Affections*, Edwards says:

> The Spirit of God is given to the true saints to dwell in them, as his proper lasting abode; and to influence their hearts, as a principle of a new nature, or as a divine supernatural spring of life and action. The Scriptures represent the Holy Spirit, not only as moving, and occasionally influencing the saints, but as dwelling in them as his temple, his proper abode, and everlasting dwelling place (I Cor. 3:16; II Cor. 6:16; John 14:6-7). And he is represented as being there so united to the faculties of the soul, that he becomes there a principle or spring of new nature and life.
>
> So the saints are said to live by Christ living in them (Gal. 2:20). Christ by his Spirit not only is in them, but lives in them; and so that they live by his life; so is his Spirit united to them, as a principle of life in them; they don't only drink living water, but this living water becomes a well or fountain of water, in the soul, springing into spiritual and everlasting life (John 4:14), and thus becomes a principle of life in them; this living water, this Evangelist himself explains to intend the Spirit of God (ch. 7:38-39).[13]

Through such imagery of water as well as sunshine and the sap of a tree, Edwards seeks to make clear the fact that the Spirit is "communicated and united to the saints." As a result, the saints are rightly "called spiritual" (pp. 200-201).

12. Jonathan Edwards, *Treatise on Grace*, in *Treatise on Grace and other Posthumously Published Writings*, ed. Paul Helm (Cambridge and London: James Clarke & Co. Ltd., 1971), pp. 58-59, 62.

13. Jonathan Edwards, *Religious Affections*, ed. John E. Smith, vol. 2, *The Works of Jonathan Edwards* (New Haven: Yale University Press, 1959), p. 200 [hereafter page citations in parentheses in the text].

Later in *Religious Affections,* Edwards says: "All gracious affections do arise from a spiritual understanding in which the soul has the excellency and glory of divine things discovered to it . . . all spiritual discoveries are transforming . . . such power and efficacy have they, that they make an alteration in the very nature of the soul." Such gracious and moral affections arise through the powerful conversion of the soul (p. 340). And thus all virtue flows forth from God's triune love, which is shed abroad in believers' hearts through the indwelling Spirit.[14]

Whether one is cognizant of it or not, Christian existence is trinitarian: God creates and redeems the saints in Christ through the Spirit. More to the point, truly Christian action is trinitarian: it flows from the triune life of God. Contrary to moralism, authentic Christian action is an overflow of God's love poured out in believers' hearts through the indwelling presence of the Spirit. This indwelling is one reason why "the saints and their virtues are called spiritual." How could it be otherwise when the Spirit of holiness "so dwells in the hearts of the saints" that they partake "of God's beauty and Christ's joy" — and so have fellowship with the Father and Son? Though the Spirit indwells Christians alone, never communicating himself to nonbelievers "in his own proper nature," nonetheless Edwards maintains that this same Spirit works in the lives of non-Christians in many ways (*Religious Affections,* pp. 200-202). Moralism fails to account for this reality, and also its flipside, namely, the very real possibility that, though people perform righteous deeds, they are not righteous, as Edwards argues of some supposed saints:

> Many anchorites and recluses have abandoned (though without any true mortification) the wealth, and pleasures, and common enjoyments of the world, who were far from renouncing their own dignity and righteousness; they never denied themselves for Christ, but only sold one lust to feed another, sold a beastly lust to pamper a devilish one; and so were never the better, but their latter end was worse than their beginning (p. 315).

14. See Danaher's discussion of this theme in *The Trinitarian Ethics of Jonathan Edwards,* pp. 144-45, 154-55.

95

The heart of the matter is the proper relationship of transformed hearts to righteous acts.

Regeneration and participation in the life of the triune God are vitally important if believers' actions are to be pleasing to God — and thus of lasting value. Though the world is full of noble people who engage in virtuous and noble acts of philanthropy, their actions do not merit eternal life or prove fully effective.[15] Such deeds are only of lasting value for those who abide in Christ through the abiding Spirit. Christ himself said (even to his disciples), "Apart from me you can do nothing" (John 15:5). Paul says — wedged between his treatment of the Spirit's gifts in 1 Corinthians 12 and 14 — that he will show the carnal Corinthians "a still more excellent way" (1 Cor. 12:31, NRSV). If one does not have love (the love of the same Spirit who gives the gifts in 1 Cor. 12 and 14), one gains nothing, regardless of the acts of philanthropy performed, even giving all of one's possessions to the poor (1 Cor. 13:3). Thus, for those interested in accomplishing mighty deeds in view of Christ, it is essential that they be vitally connected to Christ. And such a connection comes to those indwelt by his Spirit.

How, then, does the Trinity make a difference in defeating moralism? Christ's Spirit of love is powerful as it transforms and indwells human hearts. Those so indwelt by the Spirit of Christ please God as they submit to Christ and serve as holy vessels for the Spirit of love to use. Those activities that are pleasing to God come from above and flow from within. In this light, not all those who give of themselves to the poor and oppressed find favor with God, as the apostle Paul makes clear (1 Cor. 13:3), but only those quickened and captured by the Spirit of Christ's outpouring of love.

15. Gerald McDermott provides invaluable insights into how Edwards conceived of the relationship of personal spirituality to social activism, including his engagement of the public sphere. McDermott illuminates the relationship of true virtue (moving beyond moralism) to effective action (moving beyond escapism) in Edwards's thought: "Social action that did not spring from a heart captivated by God's beauty and love would be less than fully virtuous. Consequently, it would also be less than fully effective." Gerald R. McDermott, *One Holy and Happy Society: The Public Theology of Jonathan Edwards* (University Park: The Pennsylvania State University Press, 1992), pp. 180-81.

But there is more. The Trinity has a bearing on defeating escapism as well. Those who dwell in divine love with hearts of faith are pleasing to God, for the heavenly love that indwells their hearts is expansive and explosive, overflowing to earth below. While not all who give themselves on behalf of the poor and oppressed find favor with God, the inverse is true: those who find favor with God give themselves on behalf of the poor. Indeed, those who abide in Christ abandon themselves on behalf of others for Christ. They do not escape or retreat to homogeneous units to take up battle-camp positions; rather, they engage redemptively and compassionately.

Moving Beyond Escapism:
The Love-Transformed Lifestyle

I have been teaching on the theology of the affections for some years now, and students often love to have their hearts tugged and strangely warmed. But it troubles me deeply how seldom they see the connection between the overflowing, captivating love of Christ and the need for downward mobility that overturns structures and frees captives. How seldom they see the cause-and-effect relationship between the inside out and upside down aspects of Christ's kingdom! At the bottom of it all is the paradigm of cheap grace in a consumer church society: getting the spiritual goods we want at the least cost to ourselves.

Whether the evangelical subculture is conscious of it or not, the consumer spirit is deeply entrenched in its soul: that is, in many ways its soul is but a reflection of the larger culture's own narcissistic spirit. The consumer-church mindset, which offers self-gratification and fulfillment to the individual, is not "redemptive." Rather, this mindset is violent: it enslaves and violates those who have bought into it, causing them to spiral further inward and downward into the bottomless pit of their insatiable desires. The church must awaken and see itself as a peculiar people with a particular politics, a people whose mission includes shaping each other's lives through conversion and participation in the crucified body of the risen Christ. This call for upside-down living flows from an inside-out heart in which heaven dwells. Hell, on the other hand, is in hearts and lives that are turned inward and upward (as in upwardly mobile), which we can observe in some evangelical gatherings today.

Some homogeneous units that are meeting behind closed doors in suburban or exurban megachurches act out the concept of Sartre's play *No Exit*, which depicts hell as three self-consumed individuals who are locked up in a room with no escape and whose eyelids cannot close. These Christians gather there, with eyes wide open, some of them hanging out around the coffee bar to check out the possibilities for future dates, perhaps in hopes of building cozy Christian homes. Some others plan evangelistic ski trips to Vail, with the only aim of showing their non-Christian homogeneous friends that Christians can have fun, too. The predominance of this mindset in many evangelical circles today makes it very difficult to see how diabolical this orientation is, and it blinds us to the fact that by turning inward we close ourselves off to making an exit and entering into true freedom.

Those who look inward today are also often looking upward. While books that warn people not to get left behind when Christ returns may prompt some to put their homes in order and to give to the Master's cause, they may also be used by some as a stimulus to escape this world, to leave everything behind in order to build bigger homes and churches in the suburbs (or now, in the gentrified inner cities), to await that day when they are raptured to that great country club/ski resort/bistro in the sky. Can we even talk about personal holiness without also talking about holistic lifestyles?

Perhaps, on a larger American cultural scale, it all goes back to the Scopes Trial: when we fundamentalist-evangelicals fled the broader culture in waves after that trauma, we turned *inward* to cultivate our own Christian subculture and *upward* in hopes that Christ would return soon. Today, our focus on the nuclear family and the local church family in this nuclear age has replaced the focus on the in-breaking of Christ's eschatological kingdom, a kingdom that must naturally spill over from our families and churches into the broader culture around us. Given such a family-oriented religion, perhaps there is not much difference in the end between evangelicalism and Mormonism, where focusing on the family culminates in the deification of the family.

A major reason for the success of many leading evangelical churches today has to do with the fact that they give families what they want: stability and security. Stability and security are, of course, important; but if they are not properly circumscribed, they can become diabolical and idolatrous. In contrast to the inward focus and homogeneous and upwardly mobile orientation of a large segment of the Bible-believing church today, the Bible speaks of God in outwardly and downwardly mobile terms. According to Psalm 113:4-9,

> The LORD is exalted over all the nations, his glory above the heavens. Who is like the LORD our God, the One who sits enthroned on high, who stoops down to look on the heavens and the earth? He raises the poor from the dust and lifts the needy from the ash heap; he seats them with princes, with the princes of their people. He settles the barren woman in her home as a happy mother of children. Praise the LORD.

Although God gives children to barren women such as Hannah, God also wants them to dedicate their children fully to God, as Hannah did (though not necessarily for full-time Christian service). In place of cultivating family life at any cost, even at the expense of carrying the cross of Christ, the renowned American evangelical missionary Jim Elliot (1927-1956), a son, husband, and father, spoke of what following Christ would cost the family in his college journals. The same young man who wrote, "He is no fool who gives what he cannot keep to gain what he cannot lose," also wrote to his mother and requested that she pray for her children in view of Psalm 127. Young Elliot urged his mother to pray not that he and his siblings would have safe and comfortable lives, but that they would be sent forth from the quiver of God as arrows into the heart of Satan. The theological basis for his request came from the words of the psalmist: "Sons are a heritage from the LORD, children a reward from him. Like arrows in the hands of a warrior are sons born in one's youth. Blessed is the man whose quiver is full of them. They will not be put to shame when they contend with their enemies in the gate" (Ps. 127:3-5).[16]

Elliot's request was granted, and so was his mother's prayer. She and her husband would not be ashamed when their son contended in the gate with the principalities and powers. When he was martyred at the hands of the Auca Indians a few years later, Elliot's testimony and the testimonies of his slain missionary comrades were instrumental in fanning the flames among young American evangelicals for foreign missions in the second half of the twentieth century.

But Jim Elliot's perspective is largely lacking at the beginning of the twenty-first century, where many Christians come dangerously close to saying to God that their families are off-limits. It is not a matter of someone's choosing between God and family; it is a matter of dedicating one's family to God. While parents must guard against spiritual bravado and sacrificing their children to Molech for the ministry, they must also guard against the perverse spirit of hiding their children from God, and sheltering them from the world, by keeping them locked up in the Christian ghetto.[17] Children are indeed a reward and heritage from the Lord, but not as ends in themselves. Our families are to contend against God's enemies at the gates of those strongholds that Christ is tearing down, the strongholds of race and class divisions in the church. Thus, while it is important to seek to keep our children safe from harm, we must not make safety the driving force of the church's children's programs and the like. We can so shelter our children from harm that we keep them and our churches from experiencing the breaking of God's eschatological kingdom into this world in profound ways.

One Christian leader informed me that his church had determined

16. Jim Elliot, quoted in Elisabeth Elliot, *Shadow of the Almighty: The Life and Testament of Jim Elliot* (New York: Harper & Brothers, 1958), pp. 15, 131-32.

17. Mother Teresa spoke passionately of the need to protect the sanctity of children's lives for the future of the family and society. She set a profound example for us to follow by entering into the ghettos of India, not the Christian ghetto. See the script of her talk delivered at the National Prayer Breakfast, Washington, D.C., Feb. 5, 1994, in Landi Gjoni, "Mother Teresa on Family Values and Abortion Part One," 1997, http://www.drini.com/motherteresa/own_words/ (article visited on 9/7/06).

that it would not reach out to a juvenile detention facility in the area because they were afraid those youths might start attending their church and dating their daughters. A concerned parent at my own church came up to me after a sermon I gave: I had just finished preaching on the need for our church to reach out compassionately to "the least of these" in our community. This parent was worried that a lot of homeless people might begin attending our church if the leadership continued preaching this way; he urged me to make a higher priority of children's safety and not to get carried away with reaching out to those down-and-outers outside the church's doors. This advice was rather astonishing to me in view of the fact that he had just finished leading our church in a rousing set of worship songs about the need for our church members to open our hearts to reach out to those around us, especially those most in need.

While I have concerns for my children's safety and the safety of those whom they date, I must daily commit my children's lives to the Lord. I dare not stand in the way of what the Lord wants for their lives, and I do not want them to miss out on being the missional people of the missional God. A Christian lawyer friend of mine and his wife epitomize this way of thinking: they moved out of an affluent suburb and into the inner city several years ago with their daughters (their son had already grown up and had left home). Bewildered friends asked them how they could do such a thing to their daughters, wondering what kind of parents they were. My friend and his wife responded by saying that their son was the one who had missed out — that they failed him by sheltering him as a youth. Though a successful businessman, this young man had not had the profound and diverse exposure to life that their daughters have been experiencing. According to the parents, these girls have been receiving a far better preparation for participation in the twenty-first-century missional church with all the diverse challenges it faces. You can learn a lot about how healthy and spiritually awake a church is by its parents' perspectives and by its youth programs — not necessarily by the songs they sing or the doctrines they believe.

Jonathan Edwards witnessed a perverse spirit within parts of the Great Awakening of his day. His response to the problem is instructive for the church today, especially at two points. First, he warns that those given to ecstatic flights of an awakened spirit might not be so much captured by the Spirit as deluded by Satan:

> [T]hese religious affections may be carried to a great height, and may cause abundance of tears, yea, may overcome the nature of those who are the subjects of them, and may make them affectionate, and fervent, and fluent in speaking of the things of God, and dispose them to be abundant in it; and may be attended with many sweet texts of Scripture, and precious promises, brought with great impression on their minds; and may dispose them with their mouths to praise and glorify God, in a very ardent manner, and fervently to call upon others to praise him, crying out of their unworthiness, and extolling free grace. And may, moreover, dispose them to abound in the external duties of religion, such as prayer, hearing the Word preached, singing, and religious conference; and these things attended with a great resemblance of a Christian's assurance, in its greatest height, when the saints mount on eagles' wings, above all darkness and doubting . . . there may be all these things, and yet there be nothing more than the common influences of the Spirit of God, joined with the delusions of Satan, and the wicked and deceitful heart. (*Religious Affections*, p. 183)

Second, Edwards warns that piety and practice must always go together.[18] Quoting Luke 6:44, "Every tree is known by its fruit," Edwards says:

> Christ nowhere says, ye shall know the tree by its leaves or flowers, or ye shall know men by their talk, or ye shall know them by the good

18. McDermott expresses the relationship of personal piety to social expression in Jonathan Edwards this way: "Edwards's faith was not privatistic, but it was profoundly private. That is, he denounced religion devoid of social expression (privatistic) as false, but insisted that true religion emanated from a transformed heart (private). . . . Inner spiritual experience and outward religious action were movements of the same soul, pieces of the same cloth." McDermott, *One Holy and Happy Society*, p. 180. McDermott also paid attention to Edwards's negative assessment of "private" when juxtaposed to "public" (pp. 102-3); see also Jonathan Edwards, *Charity and its Fruits*, in *Ethical Writings*, ed. Paul Ramsey, vol. 8, *The Works of Jonathan Edwards* (New Haven: Yale University Press, 1989), pp. 259-61.

story they tell of their experiences, or ye shall know them by the manner and air of their speaking, and emphasis and pathos of expression, or by their speaking feelingly, or by making a very great show by abundance of talk, or by many tears and affectionate expressions, or by the affections ye feel in your hearts towards them: but by their fruits shall ye know them; the tree is known by its fruit; every tree is known by its own fruit. . . . (*Religious Affections*, p. 407)

Later he says:

Passing affections easily produce words; and words are cheap; and godliness is more easily feigned in words than in actions. Christian practice is a costly, laborious thing. The self-denial that is required of Christians, and the narrowness of the way that leads to life, don't consist in words, but in practice. Hypocrites may much more easily be brought to talk like saints, than to act like saints. (p. 411)

This quotation makes clear that Edwards had little time for a gospel of privatized affections. His view of the gospel accounts for the whole person and involves the conviction that the person whose heart has been transformed reaches out as the hands and feet of Christ to touch souls and bodies. It is a cruciform existence to which he calls believers. In *Religious Affections*, Edwards argues that while some show concern for the well-being of the "outward man" and others "pretend a great love to men's souls," the love that is truly Christian involves regard for body and soul, following the model of Christ:

But a true Christian love to our brethren, extends both to their souls and bodies. And herein [it] is like the love and compassion of Jesus Christ. He shewed mercy to men's souls, by laboring for them in preaching the gospel to 'em; and shewed mercy to their bodies, in going about doing good, healing all manner of sickness and diseases among the people. (p. 369)

Illustrating the Savior's holistic compassion for others from the Gospels, Edwards adds: "And if the compassion of professing Christians towards others don't work in the same ways, it is a sign that it is no true Christian compassion" (p. 369).

Edwards championed the popular evangelical emphasis on the transformed heart. Yet he would have distanced himself from the individualistic and otherworldly orientation of many who call themselves evangelicals today. Edwards's particular trinitarian model of the affections is quite critical of any spirituality that would prize the individual — and, by extension, the nuclear family or cell group — over the corporate, or the soul over the body. To the extent that evangelicals today, with their individualistic and relational frames of reference, fail to take up these concerns of Edwards, they make themselves out to be impostors and illegitimate children of the movement he inspired.

While evangelicals talk incessantly about personal relationships, we often reduce the relational framework and relationalism to "my kind of people," which is void of any of Jesus' concern for the neighbor. In the story of the Good Samaritan (Luke 10:25-37), Jesus defines for us what a good neighbor looks like — and who our neighbor is. Henri Nouwen defines "community" as "the place where the person you least want to live with always lives."[19] Nouwen no doubt takes his cue from Jesus, who in this story tells one of the religious leaders who his neighbor is — not necessarily someone who lives next door — and what a good neighbor looks like. Our neighbor is the person with whom we would least like to identify ourselves. Nor is it someone who is like us, or whom we like. Rather, our neighbor is a person in need, someone we encounter on the streets, and especially our downtrodden enemy and oppressor.

Jesus is the truly good Samaritan: though he was rich, he became poor so that we might become rich before God (2 Cor. 8:9). But there's more: not only is Jesus the truly good Samaritan, but he is also the person who has been beaten, robbed, and is dying, the person without shelter or a home. Thus we see Jesus both in the Good Samaritan and in the person who needs our help. We see the face of Jesus in the downtrodden

19. Henri Nouwen, "Moving from Solitude to Community to Ministry," *Leadership: A Practical Journal for Church Leaders* 16, no. 2 (Spring 1995): 83.

because he cares for the least of these, and because he has *become* the least of these. Whenever we take care of the least of these (especially fellow believers, but not exclusively so), we are taking care of Jesus (Matt. 25:40). What is required of us is a relationalism of a higher order, a trinitarian order. According to trinitarian theology, Jesus and I are only who we are in relationship to the other, including the orphan and the widow and the homeless person in distress.

God in Christ through the Spirit makes possible a world in which one can make space and time for the other, especially the dispossessed other, because God in Christ through the Spirit has made space and time for us — we who were completely other to God. For while we were still God's enemies, Christ offered himself up for us to God through the Spirit (Rom. 5:6-11; Heb. 9:14). Now God has joined us to Christ through the Spirit (Rom. 8:9-11), through whom God pours the divine love into our hearts (Rom. 5:5). And just as God goes out of himself in self-giving love through Christ in the Spirit, God takes us out of ourselves to be in communion with Christ and with one another (especially the dispossessed other) through that same Spirit's outpouring of love into our hearts. God forms us into true persons in communion, not individuals in isolation or individuals who "cell-group" themselves apart into exclusive isolation with their kind.

Jesus calls us to "embrace" in love rather than "exclude" in fear and anger those who do not belong to our niche group, to expand our circle of insiders with outsiders, rather than shrink it. Jesus informed the law expert who tried to justify himself by asking, "Who is my neighbor?" that his neighbor was the Samaritan half-breed who helped the half-dead man. By loving God and *these* neighbors, we will truly live (Luke 10:27-29, 36-37), that is, by living in the self-giving love of the triune God that Christ supremely manifested on the cross.

If we fail to take Christ's cross work seriously and fail to suffer with those who suffer and give to those in need, especially believers, we trample the Son of God underfoot. If we continue in this way, we will fall into the hands of the living God (Heb. 10:29-35). But the gravity of the situation is difficult for us to register since the spirit of the age has turned "Sinners in the Hands of an Angry God" into the seeker-friendly pop psychology of "Consumers on the Lap of a Feel-Good God."[20] We must convert structures as well as hearts.

Converting "Consumers on the Lap of a Feel-Good God" Structures

In light of the preceding discussion, we need to ask ourselves whether we are truly converted. And if we are, are we making efforts to convert the consumer-driven church and societal structures that ignore and oppress the downtrodden? Jonathan Edwards called for the restructuring of the heart as well as social relationships. Regarding the latter, he spoke prophetically against the economic injustices bound up in the market system, which was emerging as a dominant force in his day. For example, Edwards called it fraud when merchants charged more for products than was necessary for providing them with an equitable income, and he called it extortion when merchants raised the cost of items based on poverty-stricken people's dependence on such products. And far from seeing the benefits of wealth as a sign of God's favor, he claimed that God often bestows riches on those he loathes the most.[21]

He also spoke about abuses against Native Americans. His concern for holistic spirituality rooted in Christ's love in the Spirit was behind his confrontation of poverty and "the machinations of whites who wished to appropriate tribal lands" during his tenure with the Indian mission on the Massachusetts frontier.[22] He spoke against church

---

20. Tolson wonders how Edwards would view "'seeker-friendly' services" today (Tolson, "The New Old-Time Religion," p. 38).

21. See the following treatises by Edwards: "The Sin of Theft and of Injustice" and "The Peace Which Christ Gives His True Followers" in *The Works of Jonathan Edwards,* vol. 2, with a memoir by Sereno E. Dwight, revised and corrected by Edward Hickman (Edinburgh: The Banner of Truth Trust; first published, 1834; reprint, 1979), pp. 220-26 and 89-93 respectively.

22. Conforti, *Jonathan Edwards, Religious Tradition, and American Culture,* p. 2; see also McDermott, *One Holy and Happy Society,* p. 164 [hereafter page references in parentheses in text].

leaders giving the best seats in the house to the rich and powerful (McDermott, pp. 170, 181). Edwards's "ennoblement of the common Christian may have given confidence" to the people "who tried to challenge society's elites." In fact, his concern for the common Christian may well have played a role in his decision to limit access to the Lord's table to regenerate persons (McDermott, pp. 166-171, 182). While Edwards's decision to limit access to the Lord's table to those who manifested vital affections is problematical (e.g., Jesus never excluded Judas, and Paul challenged the ones in Corinth who excluded others, not those who included others), yet he did seem to recognize that the Lord's table has theo-political significance. It may well have been Edwards's attempt to reconfigure authority in the church: framing ecclesial authority in terms of poverty in spirit, not worldly wealth (McDermott, p. 171).

Unfortunately, Edwards did not apply his distinctively trinitarian model to the resolution of structural problems, at least not in the sense of calling for the restructuring of society or the development of a political theology as such.[23] In some cases, most regrettably the case of slavery, Edwards actually advanced structural problems.[24] His policies did not always live up to his trinitarian paradigm's potential, though the

---

23. McDermott says: "Edwards's call to the church to help society's poor was, of course, not revolutionary. He did not advocate structural change, but merely charity that would in the long run and in most instances probably leave the poor still poor" (McDermott, *One Holy and Happy Society*, p. 109; see also p. 181).

24. Kenneth Minkema has shown that Edwards held that, while blacks could enter into the "glorious liberty" of being God's children, they could not experience social liberty. Minkema, "Jonathan Edwards' Defense of Slavery," *The Massachusetts Historical Review* 4 (2002). http://www.historycooperative.org/journals/jah/92.1/minkema.html. Moving on from slavery, Mark Valeri has shown that, while Edwards was critical of the emerging free market in New England, he also benefited handsomely from its presence. See the following works: Mark Valeri, "The Economic Thought of Jonathan Edwards," *Church History* 60 (1991): 37-55; Valeri, "Jonathan Edwards, the Edwardsians, and the Sacred Cause of Free Trade," in D. Kling and D. Sweeney, eds., *Jonathan Edwards at Home and Abroad: Historical Memories, Cultural Movements, Global Horizons* (Columbia, SC: University of South Carolina Press, 2003). Ever the iconic figure, Edwards represents each of us as an unwitting participant in the very problem he critiques.

policies of some of his followers did.[25] Where, then, might a robust trinitarian engagement of political and social structures, as it is portrayed in Jonathan Edwards's thought, take the discussion — especially with respect to racial and class barriers in a consumer church?

Martin Luther King, Jr., another one of America's great though flawed iconic theologians, posed the same question in his own distinctive way.[26] During his student days at Crozer Seminary, King almost "despaired of the power of love in solving social problems." At that time, King thought the solution to segregation was armed conflict, not Jesus' ethic of love. He confessed: "I felt that the Christian ethic of love was confined to individual relationships. I could not see how it could work in social conflict. . . ." King's reading of Gandhi would change all that:

25. A figure like Edwards can be used in numerous ways. As Harry Stout and Kenneth Minkema have argued, "conservative" defenders of slavery, "gradualist" promoters of Africa's colonization with former slaves, and "immediatist" advocates of abolition all claimed Edwards in support of their positions. See Kenneth P. Minkema and Harry S. Stout, "The Edwardsean Tradition and the Antislavery Debate, 1790-1865," *The Journal of American History* 92, no. 1 (2005), http://www.historycooperative.org/journals/jah/92.1/minkema.html.

26. James Cone argues that Martin Luther King, Jr., is America's greatest theologian. See James Cone, "Martin, Malcolm, and Black Theology," in *The Future of Theology: Essays in Honor of Jürgen Moltmann*, ed. Miroslav Volf, Thomas Kucharz, and Carmen Krieg (Grand Rapids: Eerdmans, 1996), p. 189. While King, like Edwards, was no saint (conservative white evangelicals are often quick to point to instances of plagiarism in King's doctoral dissertation and infidelity in his marriage), he was, like Edwards, an iconic, paradigmatic figure whose theo-political framework has much to teach us. Moreover, evangelicals are often quick to point out the sins of commission of others while failing to recognize our own sins of omission. For example, evangelicals were largely absent from the civil rights protest marches of the 1960s: in the face of oppression, those who stand silently by are by no means innocent. Edwards and King were flawed men whom God nonetheless used profoundly. For a discussion of King's particular flaws, see Michael Eric Dyson, *I May Not Get There with You: The True Martin Luther King, Jr.* (New York: Touchstone, 2001); see also Richard Lischer's discussion of King's plagiarism problem in *The Preacher King: Martin Luther King, Jr. and the Word that Moved America* (New York: Oxford University Press, 1995), pp. 62-64.

As I delved deeper into the philosophy of Gandhi, my skepticism concerning the power of love gradually diminished, and I came to see for the first time its potency in the area of social reform. Prior to reading Gandhi, I had about concluded that the ethics of Jesus were only effective in individual relationships. The "turn the other cheek" philosophy and the "love your enemies" philosophy were only valid, I felt, when individuals were in conflict with other individuals; when racial groups and nations were in conflict a more realistic approach seemed necessary. But after reading Gandhi, I saw how utterly mistaken I was.

Gandhi was probably the first person in history to lift the love ethic of Jesus above mere interaction between individuals to a powerful and effective social force on a large scale. Love for Gandhi was a potent instrument for social and collective transformation.[27]

Elsewhere King says that in the earliest days of the protest in Montgomery, African-Americans were inspired, not by Gandhi, but by the Sermon on the Mount and "Christian love." Soon, however, Gandhi's method of "passive resistance" arose on the scene and achieved a position of prominence as the "technique" of the civil rights movement led by King. "Nonviolent resistance" would emerge "as the technique of the movement, while love" would stand "as the regulating ideal." According to King, "Christ furnished the spirit and motivation while Gandhi furnished the method" (*Autobiography*, p. 67). In King's words and work we can find suggestive indications of where the doctrines of Christ and the affections speak meaningfully to the engagement of structural evil.

A singular attention to the winning of souls will not get God's children to that promised land of which Dr. King spoke with such longing, hope, and conviction. Certain ecclesial structures in the African-American community assisted King in his efforts to extend beloved community beyond the African-American Christian community's church walls. Converting consumer structures inside and outside the evangelical church, as well as converting consumerist souls, is necessary if we are to realize King's dream, if the new world order is to come into

27. *The Autobiography of Martin Luther King, Jr.*, ed. Clayborne Carson (New York: Warner Books, Inc., 1998), pp. 23-24.

being, if there is to be truly one people of God — one people from different ethnicities and classes who are united in Christ by the Spirit and
united by faith.

In this chapter I have highlighted the theological strengths of the
evangelical church, namely, its emphasis on the conversion and the
transformation of the human heart and lifestyle. I have noted how important those strengths are for breaking through the race and class divisions in our land of plenty, divisions that exist in the evangelical church
as well as the country. But not only do we need to pay attention to the
triune God's transformation of the *human heart;* we also need to pay attention to the necessary transformation of *church polity configurations* in
view of the overarching conversion to a new world order. In other
words, not only do human hearts and lives need to be rearranged, but
also ecclesial structures and practices, including the reading of Scripture
and celebration of the Lord's Supper. In the next chapter I will address
church polity configurations from the standpoint of the theo-political
significance of Scripture and the sacraments as strategic resources of the
triune God in confronting this world's fallen powers, such as consumerism, racism, and classism.

CHAPTER FIVE

Reordering the Church: Recovering the Lost Ark

Realizing the Ark's Power

In the movie *Raiders of the Lost Ark,* Adolf Hitler sends his Nazi henchmen to the Middle East in search of the lost Ark of the Covenant, believing it possesses occult powers that will be of great use to its captor. But Hitler's minions are in for a rude awakening: they find to their dismay that the Ark is not something to be seized and used for one's own ambitions; instead, it consumes them, as it did the Philistines before them.

Perhaps Steven Spielberg and his fictional Hitler understand something that many churches do not: the Ark, with the enclosed commandments (Scripture) and manna (the Lord's Supper), participates in the presence of an unimaginable power (Exod. 16:33-34; 25:21-22; Deut. 10:5; Heb. 9:4), a power that intends to confront and consume race and class divisions in the church. Dependence on the Ark is largely missing in many churches today. This chapter will focus on our need to recover and restore Scripture and the sacraments (or ordinances), especially the Lord's Supper, for the purpose of confronting and consuming race and class divisions.

Restoring the Ark, Removing the Wall of Division

Colin Gunton has said that the ultimate test of the church's living out its calling is the way its witness exposes the "idolatrous perversions of

God's good creation," and the way its existence unveils the dissolution of these forces. Gunton claims that "the church's proclamation will be seen to be *merely* political unless its own *polity* is given shape by the victory of Christ on the cross."[1] In what follows I want to analyze forms of churchly action that witness to the new world kingdom order inaugurated in Christ's saving work, to which the believing church has been converted.

Without wishing to downplay the church's influence in the broader social sphere at all, I will show that the church's priority is to be shaped by Christ's victory in providing space for us to become truly creaturely — in communion with God and fellow believers. This involves the restoration of the Ark to its rightful place in Christian worship, not simply dusting off the Bible and polishing the Lord's table. The Ark restoration involves restructuring church polity around Scripture and the sacraments in order to expose and eradicate those forces that separate and divide people. While some churches have basically traded in the Ark for a coffee bar, others have simply failed to see the Ark's significance for exposing and eradicating the trade triangle forces of consumer Christianity, homogeneity, and upward mobility. Our discussion here will elaborate on how the Ark was eclipsed, how we can restore the Ark to its rightful position (highlighting the all-consuming Scripture and sacraments), and how such a restoration is important in overcoming race and class barriers in the consumer church.

Reconfiguring Our Stories in View of All-Consuming Scripture

Hans Frei speaks of the eclipse of the biblical story in modernity.[2] Modern attempts to justify Scripture's legitimacy as primarily a sourcebook for gleaning doctrinal truths (fundamentalist-evangelicalism), illustrating moral and philosophical ideals (liberalism), or bearing relevance for

1. Colin E. Gunton, *The Actuality of Atonement: A Study of Metaphor, Rationality and the Christian Tradition* (Edinburgh: T. & T. Clark, 1989), p. 183.

2. Hans W. Frei, *The Eclipse of Biblical Narrative: A Study in Eighteenth and Nineteenth Century Hermeneutics* (New Haven: Yale University Press, 1980).

practical living (seeker-sensitive Christianity) fail to convey that the Bible is the ultimate Story, the story that envelops all of our stories. We must approach the Bible, God's storied world, from the standpoint that it envelops and consumes us when we consume it.

The black church has largely bypassed the modern problem altogether, and in some respects it sustains the hermeneutic of premodern times, which saw the Bible as the ultimate and all-encompassing story of God's liberating of the world. Though that exegesis is premodern, it is for that reason all the more profound, for it is able to penetrate and participate in the primal text of liberation and salvation through the African-American community's own particular struggle. While the modern study of the Bible has helped unlock treasures old and new, it has largely failed to safeguard this overarching and participational frame of reference.

During his theological studies and early career, Martin Luther King, Jr., sought to distance himself from this tradition, only to find that he could confront the demon of segregation adequately only with the sword of the Spirit of this primitive tradition, which expounded the biblical narrative in such a way that the black struggle rose out of the storied text.[3] The metanarrative of salvation gave King's people the strength to see that their hope was greater than their oppression and that God would ultimately triumph over their pharaoh. The grand biblical story and their story within it bear witness to the missional God, who is at work in the church and society in history to bring about lasting freedom through Christ in the Spirit at the end of the age. (The African-American Christian tradition is not that of a niche group because its particularity as a distinct Christian movement was forced on it by segregation. It was not a matter of selection or choice, but, if anything, survival. Moreover, the black church's experience as a community really does serve as an analogy of the godly remnant in Scripture, which was oppressed and enslaved and looked to God for deliverance.)

Both liberal and fundamentalist critiques of such a "naïve" engagement of the text betray their own naïveté about the cultural presuppo-

---

3. See Richard Lischer, *The Preacher King: Martin Luther King, Jr. and the Word that Moved America* (New York: Oxford University Press, 1995), pp. 6-9.

sitions they bring to the Bible and to the danger they pose to an authentic African-American encounter with the inspired and inspiring Word of God. Whereas King wrestled with liberal critiques of traditional African-American approaches to Scripture, and eventually distanced himself from these critiques, many African-American Christians today have uncritically embraced fundamentalism's critique. Vincent Wimbush is astonished to observe the recent migration of many African-Americans to fundamentalist Christianity, as well as their use of fundamentalist hermeneutics to challenge biblical "illiteracy" among traditional African-American churches. His comments are instructive:

> The sharp criticism of the biblical illiteracy of African Americans is actually quite incredible. Rather than seeing in such criticism a mere reference to the lack of a certain type of education, or knowledge of the pertinent "facts," it should be interpreted as a radical religious resocialization. It amounts to a deracialization of the African American religious world view, masked, of course, as a legitimate, authoritative, and broad-based, if not universal, race-neutral view and stance. . . . Protestant-defined fundamentalism, with its obvious racial, ethnic, and class origins, was masked as a movement that had transcended all such categories through its fetishization of the Bible as text. As this fundamentalism was embraced by African Americans, African American historical cultural experiences were (depending upon the particular strain of fundamentalism or the nature of outside pressures) necessarily backgrounded, rendered invisible, or held in contempt.[4]

Conservative Christian critics of black and liberation theology often fail to acknowledge the cultural presuppositions they themselves bring to the text of Scripture. Conservative white Christians need to embrace hermeneutical humility and engage other interpretive traditions constructively if we are truly serious about moving beyond our own cul-

---

4. Vincent L. Wimbush, *The Bible and African Americans: A Brief History* (Minneapolis: Fortress Press, 2003), pp. 72-73.

tural presuppositions and getting to the true meaning of the biblical text.[5]

All traditions can benefit from a form of critical realism when they interpret the biblical text. Christians — including scholars — can never master the text, but the text, which bears witness to the triune God, can and should master them. The African-American tradition to which King returned somewhere between Montgomery and Atlanta bears witness to the revolutionary nature of Scripture, its relevance to the African-American struggle for daily bread, and its ability to speak to the loftiest philosophical and social ideals by witnessing to the narrative of Israel's God: the divine *logos* become Jewish flesh. The African-American Christian community has historically approached this revolutionary text in a dynamic of relationship and typology, knowing that the God who is revealed in Scripture is personally concerned about their plight. That community has appropriated the biblical message to its own particular situation in hopes of deliverance, and thus the community should be alarmed about the eclipse of the biblical drama, because that threatens to eclipse its own liberating hope.

The biblical drama provides hope of liberation to those minority churches often dominated by the consumer forces at work in culture today; but it also offers the hope of liberation to those dominant churches in bondage to consumerism. Jesus was so consumed by the prophetic vision that God's temple was to be a house of prayer for the nations that he was willing to lose his life to make that happen (Mark 11:17-18; John 2:16-17). Paul was so consumed by the New Testament mystery that Jewish and gentile believers could together constitute the household of God and sit together in table fellowship that he was willing to risk being ostracized for challenging Peter's homogeneous ways to make it happen (Eph. 2:11-22; Gal. 2:11-14). We must also be so consumed by the vision of all God's children feasting together at the mar-

5. On the subject of hermeneutical humility, see the conclusion to Kevin J. Vanhoozer, *Is There a Meaning in This Text? The Bible, the Reader and the Morality of Literary Knowledge* (Grand Rapids: Zondervan Publishing House, 1998); see also Grant Osborne, *The Hermeneutical Spiral: A Comprehensive Introduction to Biblical Interpretation* (Downers Grove, IL: InterVarsity Press, 1997).

riage supper of the Lamb in the future kingdom that we will do whatever it takes, here and now, to bear authentic witness to that reality (Rev. 19:6-9).

As the slave church was energized by the future hope of redemption to endure overwhelming oppression, and as William Wilberforce was energized to fight overwhelming odds for his dream of the abolition of slavery in England, the biblical hope of redemption can so energize us that we will confront and consume our homogeneous and upwardly mobile ways. At present we are so content in our affluence that we do not see how desperately we need to be delivered. As Christian Alcoholics Anonymous groups look to the Bible for lasting deliverance from consumption and addiction, we desperately need Jesus' prophetic call to us to inhabit a biblical vision so much more profound than anything our trade triangle ways have to offer. When he was exposed to the horrors of the slave trade, Wilberforce said:

> . . . so enormous, so dreadful, so irremediable did its wickedness appear that my own mind was completely made up for the abolition. A trade founded in iniquity, and carried on as this was, must be abolished, let the policy be what it might, — let the consequences be what they would, I from this time determined that I would never rest till I had effected its abolition.[6]

We need to be enlightened and consumed as Wilberforce was, so that we reconfigure our preaching in evangelicalism in view of the biblical drama — from "let my people shop and sell themselves into slavery" to "let my people go from their bondage to slavery." At the center of our church's polity, the prophetic word must replace the word that advances our profit. We need to have the words of King's famous sermon "Paul's Letter to American Christians" echo forth from evangelical pulpits

---

6. These words are taken from William Wilberforce's 1789 abolition speech recorded in the "Debate on Mr. Wilberforce's Resolutions respecting the Slave Trade," in William Cobbett, *The Parliamentary History of England. From the Norman Conquest in 1066 to the year 1803*, 36 vols. (London: T. Curson Hansard, 1806-1820), vol. 28 (1789-91), cols. 45-48.

across this land as we seek out a people captured and consumed by an expansive and life-giving vision of beloved community:

> There is another thing that disturbs me to no end about the American church. You have a white church and you have a Negro church. You have allowed segregation to creep into the doors of the church. How can such a division exist in the true Body of Christ? You must face the tragic fact that when you stand at eleven o'clock on Sunday morning to sing "All Hail the Power of Jesus' Name" and "Dear Lord and Father of All Mankind," you stand in the most segregated hour of Christian America. They tell me that there is more integration in the entertaining world and other secular agencies than there is in the Christian church. How appalling that is.[7]

We must move people with God's word on Sunday mornings to move beyond their addictions to race and class affinity groups. Authentic witness to Jesus is at stake, and we must stake our lives on it. The prophetic word of judgment always gives way to a word of hope, even if it spells the death of the prophet Moses in the wilderness on the way to the Promised Land:

> And then I got into Memphis. And some began to say the threats, or talk about the threats that were out, or what would happen to me from some of our sick white brothers.
>
> Well, I don't really know what will happen now; we've got some difficult days ahead. But it really doesn't matter with me now, because I've been to the mountaintop. And I don't mind. Like anybody, I would like to live a long life — longevity has its place. But I'm not concerned about that now. I just want to do God's will. And He's allowed me to go up to the mountain. And I've looked over, and I've seen the promised land. I may not get there with you. But I want you to know tonight, that we, as a people, will get to the promised land. And I'm

7. Martin Luther King, Jr., "Paul's Letter to American Christians," in Clayborne Carson and Peter Holloran, eds., *A Knock at Midnight: The Great Sermons of Martin Luther King, Jr.* (London: Little, Brown and Company, 1998), pp. 30-31.

happy tonight. I'm not worried about anything. I'm not fearing any man. Mine eyes have seen the glory of the coming of the Lord.[8]

The prophet may lose his life, but he gains his soul as he realizes his hope. Consumed by a nobler vision of living in light of what will be, the prophet's words of confrontation and judgment are ultimately wrapped in compassion and hope as he longs for others to join him on the journey. The call is ultimately an invitation to all God's people to gain access to a more profound reality and realize a truly prophetic dream together:

> I have a dream that one day every valley shall be exalted, every hill and mountain shall be made low, the rough places shall be made plain, and the crooked places shall be made straight and the glory of the Lord will be revealed and all flesh shall see it together. . . .
>
> With this faith we will be able to hew out of the mountain of despair a stone of hope. With this faith we will be able to transform the jangling discords of our nation [and church] into a beautiful symphony of brotherhood.
>
> With this faith we will be able to work together, to pray together, to struggle together, to go to jail together, to stand up for freedom together, knowing that we will be free one day. . . .[9]

The word of profit does not profit us nearly enough: it bankrupts our souls if not our church bank accounts. For example, a church in my area chose not to "target" a lower-income apartment complex; it passed that complex over for the more affluent housing development because of the potential financial payback for the church facilities and building program. The American church, like America in general, still has a debt to pay to those who have been long oppressed. For too long we have sent back their check marked "insufficient funds." However, the church's di-

8. King, *The Autobiography of Martin Luther King, Jr.*, ed. Clayborne Carson (New York: Warner Books, Inc., 1998), p. 365.

9. King, "I Have a Dream," in James Melvin Washington, *A Testament of Hope: The Essential Writings and Speeches of Martin Luther King, Jr.* (San Francisco: HarperSanFrancisco, 1986), p. 219 [bracketed material added].

vine bank of justice is not bankrupt.[10] The great vaults of opportunity and prosperity, the storehouses of abundance, are waiting to be opened so that we — consumed by Christ as we feast at his table, and full of the Spirit's baptism — can share generously with all God's children.

Reconfiguring Sacred Space Around the All-Consuming Sacraments

The eclipsing of the biblical drama does not end there. The same holds true for the sacraments, or ordinances, which are part of this drama: their theo-political significance has been neglected. Like prophetic preaching that confronts the powers with God's story of redemption, baptism and the Lord's Supper have important roles to play in confronting the race and class divide and restructuring the consumer church. For example, in baptism we die to our individualistic desires and privatized patterns of life as the Spirit and water consume us and as we rise anew into the arms of Christ through his body. Just as the Israelites were baptized into Moses as they crossed the Red Sea (1 Cor. 10:2), so we are baptized into Christ through water and through fire (Acts 2:38; Luke 12:49), and we bear witness to God's judgment on the fallen powers that enslave people in various ways, including trade triangles. As we are united with Christ through baptism, we undergo Christ's judgment: we suffer in him as he is judged for our sins, and we rise in victory as he judges the sin that enslaves us in his resurrection. Thus we no longer need to be enslaved to our fallen propensities and the fallen powers (Rom. 6:1-14; Col. 2:11–4:1), including base consumption and the commodifying of human identity that promote race and class divisions. While the final victory comes to us in the resurrection of our own bodies, in the meantime we live in the reality of our union with the resurrected Jesus through the Spirit (Rom. 6:1-14; 8:1-11). The Lord's Supper signifies that Christ consumes us when we consume the wafer (or loaf) and the wine (or juice) in faith.

Unfortunately, we have neutralized sacred space and watered down the sacraments' significance. According to Robert Webber, many evan-

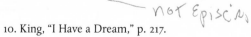

not Episc'n

10. King, "I Have a Dream," p. 217.

gelicals "sought to neutralize space" in the 1980s in order "to make the seeker more comfortable." He says: "This worked in the 1980s but is not the way to go in the postmodern world." Biblically and ethically speaking, it was not the way to go in the 1980s either. The neutralizing of the church structure (including the displacement of the font or pool and the table in many assemblies) and the negation of key dimensions of the kingdom mission, which Jesus inaugurated for the church, have minimized the power of the gospel in our lives in key ways. Those who have neutralized sacred space by displacing the baptismal font and the communion table have failed to see that these forms are not window dressing but are inseparably tied to the church's identity and kingdom mission. In response to the neutralizers, Webber cites the aptness of Marshall McLuhan's famous saying: "The medium is the message."[11] Perhaps another adage is appropriate here: birds of a certain socioeconomic and ethnic feather flock together. Has the shape of the church been changed to foster and nurture such hallowed comfort zones?

Scripture and the sacraments are constitutive of the church's identity and existence, and as such they are also bound up with the church's mission to witness to Christ's victory over the fallen powers. The central placement of the sacraments in the sanctuary and their theo-political significance for Christ's kingdom mission are a symbol of protest to modernity's devaluing of religious assemblies to what Stanley Hauerwas calls "arbitrary institutions sustained by the private desires of individuals."[12] The church, through its scriptural and sacramental existence, is that social and political dimension of the kingdom reality that bears witness to Christ's reordering of the cosmos and overcoming of the powers. Scripture and the sacraments bear witness to Christ's kingdom order, which reorders humanity in such a way as to surmount race and class divisions in the consumer church. John Howard Yoder says that, for the apostle Paul,

11. Robert E. Webber, *Ancient-Future Faith: Rethinking Evangelicalism for a Postmodern World* (Grand Rapids: Baker Book House, 1999), p. 108.

12. Stanley Hauerwas, *Against the Nations: War and Survival in a Liberal Society* (Notre Dame, IN: University of Notre Dame Press, 1992), p. 124.

... the very existence of the church is its primary task. It is in itself a proclamation of the lordship of Christ to the powers from whose dominion the church has begun to be liberated.... The church must be a sample of the kind of humanity within which ... economic and racial differences are surmounted.[13]

The very shape and structure of the church — including the space and significance awarded to the sacraments — must serve this kingdom mission and cosmic vision.

Like Martin Luther King, Maximus the Confessor, one of the church fathers, saw a close relationship between God, church, and cosmos. For his part, Maximus speaks of the church being an image of God: while composed of many, the church is also one, and it "confers" on its various members "the same divine character and title." Maximus later speaks of the church as an image of the invisible and visible universe, a microcosm, so to speak, which is "not divided in kind by the differentiation of its parts." Distinct spaces within the church, such as the sanctuary and the nave, function as sections of the whole.[14] He also observes that the immaterial and material spheres are distinct, though inseparably related:

The wise thus glimpse the universe of things brought into existence by God's creation, divided between the spiritual world, containing incorporeal intelligent substances, and this corporeal world, the object of sense (so marvelously woven together from many natures and kinds of things) as if they were all another Church, not built by hands, but suggested by the ones we build; its sanctuary is the world above, allotted to the powers above, its nave the world below, assigned to those whose lot it is to live in the senses. (Maximus, p. 69)

Maximus makes a similar comparison involving the church and the material world (p. 71).

13. John Howard Yoder, *The Politics of Jesus*, 2nd ed. (Grand Rapids: Eerdmans, 1994), p. 150.

14. St. Maximus the Confessor, *The Church, the Liturgy and the Soul of Man: The Mystagogia of St. Maximus the Confessor*, trans. Dom Julian Stead, O.S.B. (Petersham, MA: St. Bede's Publications, 1982), p. 68.

King also sees the church as a microcosm. Its structure bears witness to God's authoritative restructuring of the universe and overarching redemptive purposes. In King's church, says Richard Lischer in *The Preacher King,* one could observe the divinely appointed hierarchy that "acts as a critique of every human law and institution."[15] Power is centered in the imposing pulpit, which has an equally imposing Bible; in front of the pulpit is a humble communion table, which stands before saint and sinner seated in front of it. One's status in the church is analogous to where one sits in the congregation. The pulpit is on a stage above the congregation, and the pastor's throne just behind it. Behind the pulpit and throne sits the choir, representing the angelic host, scaling upward on a platform toward the heavens. Above and behind the choir hangs a cross, and above it a portrayal of Jesus on "colored glass" (Lischer, p. 16).

> The preacher occupies a place in the hierarchy of the divine cosmos as the one who is authorized to proclaim God's lordship over other powers. Because the preacher has been called directly by God, he also has a privileged perch outside the hierarchy as the one who can "see" how God's purposes are unfolding in the whole world. (Lischer, pp. 17-18)

King would later come to view the church — this "Afro-Baptist sacred cosmos" — as the Ark of the Covenant, which he would take with him into battle as leader of the civil rights movement. "Ebenezer's worship (and worship *space*) not only built a world for Negro survival but *institutionalized* a permanent critique of a world in which survival is all one can hope for" (Lischer, p. 17). In King's view, the sacred space of the sanctuary can be revolutionary. It stands against the principalities as a check on their powers, serving as a visible sign of God's eschatological kingdom.

While I do not embrace the hierarchical ideal of pastoral-privileged access in King's thought, or the apparent Platonic tendency in Maximus's statement, their distinctive approaches of relating the church to the cosmos do point toward the theological and theo-political significance of sa-

15. Lischer, *The Preacher King,* p. 17 [hereafter page references in parentheses in text].

cred space. In the following section I will pick up King's central insight and explore how the church's sacred space, specifically the placement and use of the Lord's table, stands as a check on the powers that promote ethnic and economic divisions in an age that is not marked by legally enforced segregation but by segregation that is nonetheless sustained through tastes, affinities, and niche selection.

Reconfiguring the Fraternal Order at the Family Feast

John Zizioulas notes that in the ancient world other groups besides the Christian church lived in loving solidarity. These fraternal orders, as they were known, involved members handing over their possessions to be shared by all. What was different about the eucharistic assembly (the church centered around the celebration of the Lord's Supper) was not its emphasis on loving solidarity but the fact that it crossed ethnic, economic, and social lines in the ancient church.[16] Some in the recent past have attempted to do the same, though — just as in the early church — it has not come without a struggle. On one occasion, the late Archbishop Oscar Romero of El Salvador brought the rich and poor together in El Salvador to celebrate the mass. Though the wealthy were incensed, Romero drew strength from the Eucharist and tried "to collapse the spatial barriers separating the rich and the poor." He did so, "not by surveying the expanse of the Church and declaring it universal and united, but by gathering the faithful in one particular location around the altar, and realizing the heavenly *Catholica* in one place, at one moment, on earth."[17]

This calls to mind Hebrews 12:

> [Y]ou have come to Mount Zion and to the city of the living God, the heavenly Jerusalem, and to innumerable angels in festal gathering, and to the assembly of the firstborn who are enrolled in heaven, and to God, the judge of all, and to the spirits of the righteous made per-

16. John D. Zizioulas, *Being as Communion: Studies in Personhood and the Church* (Crestwood, NY: St. Vladimir's Seminary Press, 1985), pp. 150-52.

17. William T. Cavanaugh, *Theopolitical Imagination* (Edinburgh: T. & T. Clark, Ltd., 2002), p. 122 [hereafter page references in parentheses in text].

fect, and to Jesus, the mediator of a new covenant, and to the sprin-
kled blood that speaks a better word than the blood of Abel. (Heb. 12:
22-24, ESV)

The profound typology and verbal iconography in the book of Hebrews
is often lost on modern-day Christians. (I use "typology" here to refer to
those Old Testament persons, images, and events that foreshadow
Christ and his work, figures such as Moses, Aaron, and the "old covenant" sacrificial system; "verbal iconography" means verbal pictures
through which we perceive divine realities.) Also lost is the profound
iconography of the Lord's Supper, which, like the book of Hebrews,
beckons us to enter and experience again and again the storied world of
salvation history centered in Christ and mediated through the Spirit to
all the saints.

The Lord's Supper bears witness to Christ's transforming, saving
work whereby he overcomes ethnic and economic divisions of space
and time, including those fostered by the consumer church. Regardless
of how one views Christ's presence in the elements, the Lord's table is a
special place for meeting Christ and bringing one another together —
haves and have-nots alike. One wonders about the possible connection
between churches given to upwardly mobile, homogeneous tendencies
and their infrequent celebration of and lack of attention to the Lord's
Supper. Christian niche churches unwittingly function more as fraterni-
ties than they do as the body of Christ.

The Lord's Supper is as much about the real presence of Christians
to one another as it is about the real presence of Christ to believers. Yet,
given the privatization of spirituality and the minimizing of religious
symbolism in America, people often have difficulty discerning the potency of religious symbols and their potential for effecting social change
(Cavanaugh, p. 83). The church is often reduced to a voluntary association of fervent and pious individuals whose public existence is constituted by state and society, benign or malevolent. In contrast, Jesus the
living Word, the Spirit, Scripture, baptism, and the Lord's Supper are
what truly make the church the church, constituting it and its polity as a
distinctive political and public entity.

This view of the Lord's Supper adds new meaning to the old saying "you are what you eat." By feasting on the body and blood of Christ together in faith and through the Spirit, we go deeper into the reality of our participation in Christ and one another. Paul warns the Corinthians against participating in both the table of demons and the table of the Lord: "The cup of blessing that we bless, is it not a participation in the blood of Christ? The bread that we break, is it not a participation in the body of Christ? Because there is one bread, we who are many are one body, for we all partake of the one bread" (1 Cor. 10:16-17, ESV). In Christ by faith and through the Spirit, the blessed Scripture and the Lord's Supper serve to bring the Christian family together as one around the table (see also Cavanaugh's discussion, p. 93). When we partake of the cup and wafer, the chalice and loaf, God beckons us to enter and participate all the more fully, looking toward that day when faith will become sight and we will eat together at our own wedding feast with the Lamb. Though we are now poor and crippled, blind and lame, spotted and filthy, we will then be made whole and holy.

Some churches may come to sense that something is missing in their worship services and may embrace the Lord's Supper as making a significant contribution to church life, especially as it challenges individualism's disruptive tendencies and modernity's dismissal of sacred symbols. However, progressive churches given to upward mobility and homogeneity may use the Lord's Supper to promote their fraternal orders of healthy and holy people in the here and now, given their own tendencies, which run counter to God's redemptive purposes in Christ. Even worse, perhaps, such churches may highlight the Lord's Supper (along with incense) as a marketing ploy to appeal to consumers with a more symbolic and sacramental frame of mind.

A consumer heart is in danger of being destroyed by the disease of its own consumption. Reconfiguring church space and rearranging furniture presuppose reconfiguring the heart, and those actions also have an impact on our patterns of behavior and practice. Congregations must be very intentional about deconstructing ideological structures that have generated religious segregation. At least in Corinth the have-nots attended the same churches as the haves did. Today the have-nots do not simply stand outside in the courtyard during the "love feasts." The church is often structured in such a way that the have-nots do not feel truly welcome to attend. Fundamentalist-evangelical churches that were once outside the city gate, bearing Christ's shame — or so it appeared — have fought their way back inside the system through their strategic movement from retreating fortresses to stationary battle camps and homogeneous units. But they have done very little to bring true outsiders inside beyond running rescue missions and homeless shelters (important work in its own right). There must be an authentic, intentional struggle to convert church structures themselves in order to reach out, not retreat, and make all outsiders welcome if the church is to be truly faithful to God's kingdom purposes.

This missional orientation will include greater attention to what we wear and how we relate to the community around our church if we wish to have a sacramental and salt-and-light presence in the community. While it is certainly true of many "white" churches, I know of an African-American church in the inner city that is made up of middle-class commuter members who have virtually no connection with the community around their church. Members moved their families out of the community some time before for greener pastures as they became more affluent; now they come back only for Sunday morning worship services, and they are always very well dressed. The inner-city blacks and whites who have remained in the neighborhood cannot relate to them. An Anglo friend of mine who moved into that neighborhood and attended the church for some time told me that he had invited a black woman from the neighborhood several times to visit the church. Finally, she agreed to go to his church with him. But when he went to pick her up that Sunday morning, he had to wait for some time as she tried to make herself presentable. She finally appeared in a dress, but it didn't fit her. He could tell that she felt very awkward and uncomfortable, apprehensive that she would not fit in with their "dress code" and could not meet their social expectations. She never attended the church again. The problems we face are not simply white and black, but green as well (the separations of cash and class).

The same basic point about authenticity and intentionality and integrity could well be made of established and traditional mainline white churches. The Lord's Supper is not a panacea or cure-all for overcoming race and class divisions. Traditional mainline parish churches have featured the Lord's table in their houses of worship, but they have often paid lip service to its theo-political significance by simply going through the motions of eating and drinking together at the meal with the have-nots. Intentionality, integrity, and strength through weakness are required of all churches celebrating and practicing the Lord's Supper as designed by God. What Marva Dawn says in the context of challenging church-growth strategies applies universally:

> To live "the breaking of bread" with congregational integrity — without any barriers between peoples, without any segregations based on economics, race, or musical style — demands great weakness. Many of the church marketing gurus advocate churches of homogeneity, appealing to those who are like us so that our churches will grow, but this violates the sacrament of Christ's presence and destroys our testimony to the world that there are no divisions and distinctions among the people of God.[18]

God must break us as we break the bread to break through our race and class divisions.

The god Mammon has a subtle impact on the church, making it incredibly difficult to confront the disparities that exist in Christian communities. These disparities keep some outsiders outside the church because they cannot keep up with the Joneses in church, let alone the ones down the street. Like Elmer Gantry, such outsiders know all too well that many church members believe "poverty is blessed, but . . . bankers make the best deacons."[19] The desire to make favorable impressions on one's peers by wearing expensive clothes and building expensive churches wages war against the need to foster a community of economic redistribution. All of this is bound up with what Dawn calls "a spiraling cause-

18. Marva J. Dawn, *Powers, Weakness, and the Tabernacling of God* (Grand Rapids: Eerdmans, 2001), p. 98.
19. Sinclair Lewis, *Elmer Gantry*, Signet Classic Edition (New York: Penguin Books, 1927), XVII.1, p. 230.

and-effect dialectic" (p. 115), which increases the rapacity of consumer cravings and decreases the opportunity to overcome the divide. (An aside: one way to safeguard America's economy while also nurturing economic redistribution in the church would be for a person to buy two suits, dresses, or designer shirts of the same price — one for himself or herself and one for a person who would like to attend church but does not because he or she can't live up to the unspoken dress standard.) Dawn plays the part of a prophetess when she says:

> For there to be a new creation, the old self must know its weakness and die to its own prejudices, tastes, class structures, and personal desires. How can we share this eschatological feast if we don't participate in displaying God's future, in which all will be equally fed and we will all join together in universal praise? It seems to me that if we eat the body and blood of Christ in expensive churches without care for the hungry, the sacrament is no longer a foretaste of the feast to come, but a trivialized picnic to which not everyone is invited. (Dawn, p. 99)

The early church struggled with the same phenomenon. While the consumer ideology and church-growth strategies, based on taste and preference, are modern phenomena, greed is not. The Corinthian church could pass for a kissing cousin of many American congregations: Paul laments the fact that the Corinthian Christians are turning the Lord's Supper into an orgiastic feeding frenzy.

> When you come together, it is not really to eat the Lord's supper. For when the time comes to eat, each of you goes ahead with your own supper, and one goes hungry and another becomes drunk. What! Do you not have homes to eat and drink in? Or do you show contempt for the church of God and humiliate those who have nothing? What should I say to you? Should I commend you? In this matter I do not commend you! (1 Cor. 11:20-22, NRSV)

I rarely hear these verses read at the celebration of the Lord's Supper. The verses that immediately follow this passage are cut out of context and transposed into another key: "For I received from the Lord what I also handed on to you . . ." (NRSV). Perhaps one could argue that these verses are not read in most churches because most churches do not celebrate the love feast. But, regardless of what we make of the love feast, we should still read these verses when celebrating the Lord's Supper because of their direct message concerning the current economic disparity that is manifest in dress codes and attitudes in the church. Indeed, it would be very meaningful to enact this Pauline text by celebrating the love feast: it vividly highlights the biblical importance of communion for Christians, and it also sheds light on the unbiblical economic disparity and divisions among Christians.

Church practices, including spatial configurations such as the placement of the table and the baptismal font, bear witness to or detract from Christ's atoning work and the moral space it creates. One way or another, the church performs stories that reconfigure or rearrange our use of space. How, then, can the church reconfigure space to bear witness to God's saving work in Christ? One small thing one church has done is place the communion table front and center in the sanctuary (it was off to the side in weeks when it was not in use) so that it gains greater prominence during the worship celebration. In addition, on one particular communion service Sunday, at the close of the sermon those leading worship asked the people to go downstairs to the fellowship hall to take communion while sitting at tables with those with whom they do not normally associate. They read from 1 Corinthians 11, including Paul's rebuke concerning the divisions among them based on negative cultural patterns of consumption. They also asked that someone at each table break the loaf of bread and that each person speak about the significance of Christ in his or her life. After each person had spoken, all of the people at the table broke off a piece from the loaf, dipped it in the cup at the center of each table, and ate it. Many people commented afterwards that they appreciated the opportunity to restructure their group dynamics. The Lord's Supper could also be celebrated in this manner at a church potluck to which every member would bring a dish for all to share.

These are small steps, but they are concrete steps. As our churches put their houses in order by pursuing loving solidarity for overcoming

129

race and class divisions, not simply rearranging the furniture and playing musical chairs, they will be in a position to conquer consumerism and niche selection within their walls, and they will bear witness to society at large that there is more to life than what consumer selection has to offer.

We must also remind each other that the church comes together as a family at the Lord's table, just as the nuclear family comes together at the family meal. The Lord's Supper cultivates and intensifies believers' communion as a family centered around Christ, who is its head. The word of thanksgiving and the breaking of bread accepted in faith confers the same divine quality on all as members of God's family. Jesus is the head of "a community of consumption."[20] In place of consuming humans *(homo consumens)*, Christians become increasingly consumed people *(homo consumendus)* through their deepening communion with Christ at the Lord's family feast. Christ consumes them even as they consume him through faith in the Spirit, intensifying their participation in his body in concrete space and time and overcoming the barriers between themselves and others.[21] This dynamic reality of relationship signifies enlightened consumption involving people in communion from different walks of life rather than individuals or affinity groups in their own insularity.[22]

When we dine with Christ, we also commune with his body; for, as head of the church, Christ is never apart from his body (Col. 1:18). We should always approach the table mindful of the *body* of Christ — that is, those gathered with us; it is also important to note that the whole church is gathered together at each assembly, not just part of it (1 Cor. 1:2; 2 Cor. 1:1).[23] Christ is united to all believing communities through the Spirit,

20. John Howard Yoder, *Body Politics: Five Practices of the Christian Community before the Watching World* (Nashville: Discipleship Resources, 1992), p. 17.

21. See Cavanaugh, *Theopolitical Imagination*, p. 47.

22. John Zizioulas also contrasts individuals in isolation with persons in communion. In Zizioulas's work, the individual in isolation is bound up with the biological hypostasis whereas the person in communion concerns the ecclesial and eschatological hypostasis. See Zizioulas, *Being as Communion*.

23. See the related discussion by a Baptist theologian, Millard J. Erickson, *Christian Theology*, vol. 3 (Grand Rapids: Baker Book House, 1985), p. 1033.

and together they make up his body. Thus, if Christ is present, the whole church is present in a given location. These theological truths should influence our social etiquette, so that we do not hoard God's bounty to ourselves or in our individual churches.

Christ calls us to set aside our personal grievances toward one another and move beyond our affinity groups as brothers and sisters in Christ. We can choose our friends, but not our siblings. And so it is with the church: we didn't choose the people who would come into God's family, but Christ chose us just as he chose them. The head of the body's blood running through us is thicker than our affinities, and he expects us to share the meal with all our brothers and sisters. Those gathered at family reunions reminisce about days gone by, and the same holds true for God's people when they gather together at the meal. As the Israelites were instructed to retell the grand story of redemption during their Passover celebrations (Exod. 12:14-28), so it is with the church (1 Cor. 11:23-26). The angel of death passed over the homes of Israel on the night it passed judgment on the pharaoh, the night Israel fled from its slavery in Egypt. The tribes of Israel fought together to inherit the land God promised them, and every year during the Passover celebration Israel remembered God's faithfulness to them in calling them out of Egypt and into the Promised Land.

We are to reminisce at the table, just as the Israelites did at their family tables, recounting what God has done for us in freeing us from bondage as we seek the inheritance God has promised us. The people of Israel went forth in the footsteps of the nation's father, Abraham, and its deliverer, Moses. They went in search of a country and a city whose foundations are from God (Heb. 11:8-16, 24-29, 39-40). We look forward to the day when that city — Christ's bride, the church (Rev. 21:2-3; Eph. 5:25-33) — is displayed in all its glory, and God dwells in our midst (Rev. 21:3). On its gates are written the names of Israel's twelve tribes, and on its foundations are written the names of the twelve apostles (Rev. 21:12-14). "The kings of the earth will bring their splendor into" that city, and "the glory and honor of the nations will be brought into it" (Rev. 21:24, 26).

The people of Israel were nourished on the manna (Exod. 16) and the water from the rock (Exod. 17:1-7; Num. 20:1-13) on their journey. Scripture tells us that Christ is that rock and the true manna from heaven

(1 Cor. 10:4; John 6:25-59). The walls of Jericho fell before God's people carrying the Ark, uniting the prostitute Rahab with the other people of faith (Josh. 6; Heb. 11:30-31), just as the walls of division fall before the Ark today, uniting repentant prostitutes and tax collectors with all the other saints as brothers and sisters, as we go in search of the city of God.

Christ beckons us to the table, and then he sends us out. The missional God reconfigures and replenishes us so that we can overcome the forces arrayed against us and build beloved community inside and outside the church's walls. We do not fight against flesh and blood, but against the fallen powers in the heavenly realms (Eph. 6:12), the masters of the consumer Balrog. God exhorts us to care for our wounded and not leave them behind, to care for orphans and widows in their distress, and to give asylum to the foreigner who would join us on our journey to the Promised Land.

The biblical pageant and the Passover celebration provide an iconic picture within which we can place ourselves. This same pageant and Passover celebration should also inspire various churches to move beyond their tribalistic agendas and become partners with other "tribes" to break down the consumer walls that divide us and build firmly on the church's foundations in the Promised Land. We must care for the welfare of other churches as well as the welfare of the cities across the land, waiting for that day when the kings of the earth and the nations will bring their splendor and glory and honor into the church — the city of the New Jerusalem.

Recovering Lost Civilization through the Ark

In this chapter I have focused on Scripture and the sacraments, especially the Lord's Supper, as vehicles for restructuring church life to bring people together from different backgrounds, including different ethnicities and economic levels. The need of the hour is to recover lost community through the Ark of the Covenant in a consumer culture. Like Israel, the church is on the move: taking hold of the Ark, it battles with those forces that would keep it from entering the Promised Land. Each church needs solidarity among believers of all walks of life, and the body of Christ needs solidarity among the churches (tribes). We must take hold of the Ark and go beyond the confines of the church and become partners with those "nations" who will be our allies, as they were with Israel, in order to bring peace to the land.

The Ark not only serves to restore lost community. It also strengthens us in the struggle to recover lost civilization. I have mentioned Martin Luther King's visualizing the "Afro-Baptist sacred cosmos" as the Ark of the Covenant that he would take with him into battle as leader of the civil rights movement in search of the Promised Land. King brought the prophetic structuring of the church to bear on building civil society, even using Christ's love of the enemy (to which the Lord's Supper bears witness) as a form of civil disobedience to achieve it, though it meant that he would eventually die in the wilderness.

In the next chapter I will discuss more fully the ways in which Christians can confront the consumer church and culture with the Ark in hopes of reconciling those of different ethnic and economic backgrounds. The church with its Ark (Scripture and the Lord's Supper) is not a retreating battle camp but an advancing, redemptive force. Christ demands not only reconciliation but also the redistribution of the bounty of the table as the missional church goes out across the land. Christians and churches must relocate and redistribute the bounty of the Lord's table, taking the Ark of the Covenant throughout the region in solidarity with other churches and with our whole society to build the beloved community.

CHAPTER SIX

Reordering the Church's Outreach: Overcoming Market Forces and Building Beloved Community

Faith-Based Emporiums and the Communal, Co-missional Church

In one episode of *The Simpsons*, their church building burns down, and the Simpsons and their fellow church members sell their collective soul to the devil (in this case, the nuclear power plant owner) to finance the church's building program. They end up turning the church into a "faith-based emporium" equipped with a money-changing booth, a pulpit with a screen projecting advertisements, and plush theater seats for one's viewing pleasure.

This *Simpsons* episode satirizes the problem of how consumerism co-opts the drive for church stability and growth. In the struggle for survival, which in turn requires cultural relevance and marketing savvy, churches are severely tempted to cater to people who choose churches and programs that give them the spiritual "goods" they want when they want them, and at the least cost to themselves. This puts a lot of pressure on church leaders to deliver those goods.[1] If church leaders do not meet consumer expectations, they risk losing their consumers to the church

---

1. See Philip D. Kenneson and James L. Street, *Selling Out the Church: The Dangers of Church Marketing* (Nashville: Abingdon Press, 1997; reprint, Eugene, OR: Cascade Books, 2003), for an important critique of the theological presuppositions behind the church-marketing paradigm.

on the other side of the subdivision. In this chapter I want to appeal to churches — the communal and co-missional people of God — to overcome the market forces that foster race and class divisions by becoming partners with other churches and the broader society to build a beloved community. As pointed out by the American culture critics who are the writers/producers of *The Simpsons,* this is no easy task in an age of the faith-based emporium.

The contributors to the book *Missional Church* claim that many people, both inside and outside the church in North America, "expect the church to be a vendor of religious services and goods," as George Hunsberger puts it.[2] This vendor orientation stands in marked contrast to the Bible's description of the church as the temple of the Holy Spirit (1 Cor. 3:16), the people of God (1 Pet. 2:10), God's family or household (Eph. 2:19-22), and the body and bride of Christ (Eph. 5:29-32). In fact, a vendor-minded, commodity-oriented Christianity stands as the polar opposite of the New Testament vision for a church of integrity and unity. For one thing, it is divisive — and at several levels. For example, a commodity-oriented model of the church separates churches from their members (Hunsberger, p. 85). In addition, a commodity-oriented model of the church separates churches from each other: churches are in competition to deliver the best goods — and to deliver those goods in a more digestible format than their competitors do. It is a dog-eat-dog world in the church, as Roger Finke and Rodney Stark argue: "Where religious affiliation is a matter of choice," as it has been in America since the earliest days of the republic, "religious organizations must compete for members and . . . the 'invisible hand' of the marketplace is as unforgiving of ineffective religious firms as it is of their commercial counterparts."[3] Furthermore, a commodity-oriented model of the church separates churches according to race and class by catering to consumer desires for homogeneity and upward mobility. This

2. George R. Hunsberger, "Missional Vocation: Called and Sent to Represent the Reign of God," in Darrell L. Guder, ed., *Missional Church: A Vision for the Sending of the Church in North America* (Grand Rapids: Eerdmans, 1998), p. 84.

3. Roger Finke and Rodney Stark, *The Churching of America, 1776-1990: Winners and Losers in Our Religious Economy* (New Brunswick: Rutgers University Press, 1992), p. 17.

consumerist orientation furthers the long-standing propensity in American life to form churches and denominations along race and class lines.[4]

Over against a commodity-oriented, church-growth model of the church, Christians today need a communal and co-missional model, a model that envisions the church as made up of its qualitative relationships and that pursues partnerships in breaking down divisions between peoples. Such a model finds its basis in the life and heart of the non-homogeneous, triune God, who exists as Father, Son, and Spirit in perfect communion. This non-homogeneous, communal God is also co-missional. For the Father pours out his downwardly mobile love into the world through the sending of the Son and Spirit. Moreover, this communal God invites us to collaborate in this trinitarian mission and encourages us to become partners with one another, and encourages churches to become partners together as well. The church is created in the image of this communal and co-missional God, and so its own being is a being in communal procession (see also Hunsberger's discussion, p. 82). The aim is to unite churches and their members, to unite churches to each other locally and globally, and to unite races and classes in the church and beyond.

The Lord's Supper bears witness to this communal and co-missional orientation. And the Holy Spirit, who lifts our hearts up to Christ, who is seated at the Father's right hand, pours us out into the world at the conclusion of the celebration of the Lord's Supper. This bears witness to our participation in Christ' life, for Christ poured his own life out for the world after the Last Supper in order to break down divisions between God and humanity, Jew and gentile, male and female, slave and free. Through the Spirit, God invites us to experience, in our celebration of the Lord's Supper, a foretaste and foreshadowing of Christ's wedding banquet in the eschatological kingdom, where there

---

4. See H. Richard Niebuhr, *The Social Sources of Denominationalism* (New York: H. Holt & Co., 1929), where he argues that class differentiation rather than doctrinal disagreement is the dominant reason historically for the plethora of denominations and other religious groups in America.

will be no divisions or shortages in the community of God, for all will
partake liberally and lovingly.

In view of this eschatological vision, the church must resist treating
members as though they are potential consumers, selling impersonal religious commodities and commodifying relationships. Rather than dol-
ing out sacramental grace on demand, the people of God are called to
celebrate interpersonal communion through the feast and to proclaim
that communion to the world. Energized and empowered by this meal,
they are called to proclaim Christ's victory over the powers. They are
called to relocate, reconcile, and redistribute the Lord's bounty. The
church can thus overcome the market forces that commodify humans
and destroy communion, and it can create beloved community in their
place. What is this particular form of ecclesial engagement? We begin
with the call to build beloved community.

The Call to Build Beloved Community:
The Rebinding Work of Shalom

Just as Martin Luther King took his church (his Ark of the Covenant)
with him to fight his civil rights battles in solidarity with others, as in the
famous bus boycott, churches must become partners together in solidarity as they carry forward their symbolic Ark: Scripture and the Lord's
Supper. King's holistic perspective of bearing witness to Christ's kingdom in the church and the world encapsulates the heart of biblical religion, which involves the rebinding work of shalom. Quentin Schultze
defines religious activity in this holistic way:

> [T]o act religiously in the world is to rebind the broken cosmos. Reli-
> gion addresses the most fundamental issues faced by all peoples in all
> times — issues of brokenness, healing, and ultimately reconciliation.
> The purpose of religion is to reveal to people how they become recon-
> ciled to each other, to themselves, to the physical world, and to
> God. . . . Living a religious life means being committed to the rebind-
> ing of both private self and public life, to humbly serving one's neigh-

bor rather than merely to exploiting markets, building new organizations, or discovering technological innovations.[5]

The church must see its task as a truly religious one: to seek the healing of the personal and public spheres of life before God. This communal and co-missional view of the Christian religion and the church entails rebinding broken lives, churches, and the world — including confronting race and class divisions both inside and outside the consumer church. That view stands in marked contrast to a view of the church as a stationary location where religious consumer goods and services are offered to waiting customers who wish to satisfy their privatized religious appetites and affections, a place that intensifies the divisions.

Contrary to this stationary notion of the church, God sends the church out into society with the Ark to witness to the divine rebinding, reconciling, and redemptive activity in the world. This mobile model of the church is corroborated by Jesus' portrayal of his followers in the Gospels: they are to make disciples themselves as they go on their way (Matt. 28:19), and the gates of hell will not prevail against them (Matt. 16:18). These two texts indicate that the apostolic community is truly one that is on the move — both a sent and sending community. Borne along by the bread and wine and bearing the sword of the Spirit, the church is sent into society to witness to the victory we gain in the crucifixion, resurrection, ascension, and return of Christ.

Like Martin Luther King, John M. Perkins conceives of God's reconciling community as a people on the move. The connection between the civil rights movement championed by King and the community development movement led by Perkins is described by Charles Marsh. While the beloved community in the form of King's civil rights movement fell prey to "fragmentation and disillusionment" after his death, it reemerged through the "more modest, yet more enduring" work of Perkins, who took up King's mantle and moved forward in establishing beloved community by promoting race reconciliation, economic prog-

5. Quentin J. Schultze, *Habits of the High-Tech Heart: Living Virtuously in the Information Age* (Grand Rapids: Baker Academic, 2002), p. 72.

ress, and the transformation of local communities in disrepair.[6] Perkins grounds this "more modest, yet more enduring work" in his Christian Community Development Association's principles of relocation, reconciliation, and redistribution.[7] I want to adapt Perkins's three principles in this chapter and apply them to the life of the church as a whole in view of the Lord's Supper. I will conceive of reconciliation as a rebinding of a broken world and Christian community by means of relocation and the redistribution of need, responsibility, resources, ownership, and glory.

Reconciliation and Relocation

One way the communal and co-missional church of the triune God goes mobile and relocates is through the Lord's Supper. The Supper illuminates and intensifies the profound reality of participation: the whole church is present in each assembly, and each local assembly is present in the whole through Christ, their head. In its own community and beyond, each church is to exist for the whole church. Healing a broken church and world means that individual church ministries need to get beyond their church walls, and the Lord's Supper helps relocate churches. It helps break down the walls and spaces that divide them, which helps them realign themselves toward mission for the greater good of the whole church, including the breaking down of divisions between "Jews" and "gentiles," "bond" and "free," rich and poor. This mobility and wall-breaking suggests a kind of permeability between churches.

A distinct though analogous permeability exists in the church's relationship with the surrounding society. William Cavanaugh says that the person who consumes the Lord's Supper "begins to walk in the strange landscape of the body of Christ, while still inhabiting a particular

---

6. Charles Marsh, *The Beloved Community: How Faith Shapes Social Justice, from the Civil Rights Movement to Today* (New York: Basic Books, 2005), pp. 4-5.

7. John M. Perkins, *With Justice for All*, with a foreword by Chuck Colson (Ventura: Regal Books, 1982); see the section entitled "The Strategy," which includes chs. 6-18.

earthly place." The universal body of Christ enters into concrete local space and transforms it, meaning that, as we partake of the Lord's Supper — engaging Christ in our union with him — Christ takes us to where he is in the world. "Turn the corner, and the cosmic Christ appears in the homeless person asking for a cup of coffee. Space is constantly 'interrupted' by Christ himself, who appears in the person of the weakest, those who are hungry or thirsty, strangers or naked, sick or imprisoned (Matt. 25:31-46)."[8] Christ's mobility and the permeability of space signified by the Lord's Supper suggest that the church, which is his body, has a responsibility to the larger social sphere.

The church is to function as a preservative in society. In many quarters, however, the American evangelical church is like salt that has lost its saltiness and has failed to preserve the Lord's Supper's savory significance for daily life; thus it risks being thrown out and trampled under foot (Matt. 5:13). Eleven o'clock on Sunday morning is still the most segregated and divisive hour of the week: there is little unity among churches, which can be seen in the ecumenical divisions in general and the race and class divisions in particular. And the current commodity-market church has exacerbated these divisions. One vital means to confront this divide is for the church to pay greater attention to the Lord's Supper and what it signifies as the breaking of Christ's body and outpouring of his blood to rebind and make individuals and communities whole.

On the individual level, we as believers must certainly examine ourselves before the Lord's table and repent of the roles we have played in advancing and reinforcing race and class divisions in Christ's body. But our self-examination must extend to the corporate sphere as well: it should include critical examination of the divisions between churches in a given city, town, suburb, subdivision, and region. Those divisions defy the New Testament's identification of the church with a given locale — the churches in Smyrna, Philadelphia, and Colossae, for example. Even if they were small, emergent house churches originally, the early church

8. William T. Cavanaugh, *Theopolitical Imagination* (Edinburgh: T&T Clark, 2002), p. 120.

set up leadership posts in key cities. Theirs was a model for our time: they followed the mandate of solidarity among churches and solidarity on behalf of the community at large. The overriding tendency of many denominations, dioceses, and megachurches is to function as fiefdoms unto themselves, corporate entities set off from other churches. But true churches — if they are to follow the model of the early church — must see themselves as sending and being sent to all churches in the region.

Self-examination involving the Lord's Supper should also include close attention to church locations and church building programs. A church's building program serves as a spiritual barometer of how well that church understands its missional vocation and how much it strives for unity in the larger body of Christ and in the community. But the location of church buildings and ministries also suggests something of the mobility and ministry one might seek there: if churches are to serve as preservatives rather than as Prozac in the society, they must cultivate a visible and vital presence in the heart of the broader community, just as believers themselves should be mobile, should shake themselves "out of the saltshaker and into the world," as Rebecca Pippert has put it.[9]

In "Sacred Spaces: Designing America's Churches," Gretchen Buggeln says: "In what congregations build and where they build it, they say something about their relationship to the surrounding culture. They also demonstrate what is important in their rituals and beliefs. . . . Intentionally or not, buildings communicate what really matters to their builders."[10] Nineteenth-century auditorium churches were not intended to serve as remote spiritual retreat centers; rather, they were shaped by an aim to serve a very public role in society — extending far beyond the church walls.[11]

---

9. Rebecca Pippert, *Out of the Saltshaker and into the World: Evangelism as a Way of Life*, rev. ed. (Downers Grove, IL: InterVarsity Press, 1999).

10. Gretchen T. Buggeln, "Sacred Spaces: Designing America's Churches," *Christian Century*, June 15, 2004, p. 25.

11. See Jeanne Halgren Kilde, *When Church Became Theatre: The Transformation of Evangelical Church Architecture and Worship in Nineteenth-Century America* (Oxford: Oxford University Press, 2002).

How do current auditorium churches compare to their nineteenth-century counterparts? Buggeln closes her article by saying that it is very difficult to discern the architecture's meaning — that insight often comes with hindsight. But she urges us to be alert to the message church architecture sends "about the place of religion in our lives and in our communities." She then raises several questions about the look-alike shopping mall megachurches, and one of her questions goes to the heart of our focus in this chapter: "Can a church built in the idiom of a secular consumer society effectively counter that culture's influences?" While some may argue that Buggeln's claim does not account for the inherent multiplicity of meanings of all symbols, her claim reveals that, at the very least, look-alike shopping-mall churches send mixed signals (Buggeln, p. 25).

What should be made of the largest, most successful churches, those cities unto themselves that rise above idyllic landscapes, shopping-mall castles far removed from the grime of urban life? Do they convey inordinate consumption and a striking sense of isolation? What role do they envision playing in the war against homogeneity and upward mobility? Are these churches involved in the fight against race and class divisions, or do they promote those divisions — intentionally or unintentionally?

That the whole Christ (*totus Christus*) is present to each assembly in every location where the celebration of the Lord's Supper bears witness should awaken each assembly to be concerned for the total church in a given region, not just for those physically present. It also suggests that these churches should work together for the common good of Christ's kingdom in that region (rather than using social-justice initiatives, for example, as marketing techniques to draw "needy" consumers to their particular programs). Unfortunately, though, too often the church has had a Jonah complex, wishing God to judge society rather than redeem it. Too often the church has focused its attention on taking care of the hedges around the building and has failed to lift up its eyes and look beyond its lot. God's response to Jonah is apt here:

> You are concerned about the bush, for which you did not labor and which you did not grow; it came into being in a night and perished in

a night. And should I not be concerned about Nineveh, that great city, in which there are more than a hundred and twenty thousand persons who do not know their right hand from their left, and also many animals? (Jonah 4:10-11, NRSV)

A given congregation's concept of the church, its sphere of engagement, its heart of compassion, and its view of Christ must be as big as the region. Each church must intentionally reframe its sense of place and must guard against fleeing to the fringes of society. Personal and ecclesial self-examination for the sake of reconciliation in view of the Lord's Supper will lead to relocation, which will involve a repositioning of ministry vision and will also lead to redistribution.

Reconciliation and Redistribution

Reconciliation involves redistribution. Here I will discuss five aspects of redistribution: redistribution of need, responsibility and blame, resources, ownership, and glory.

Reconciliation and the Redistribution of Need

First, self-examination that involves reconciliation and redistribution entails the redistribution of need. This means that a humble spirit of giving and receiving will replace the haughty spirit of charity and snobbery toward the poor. All who partake of the common cup testify to this shared need. A conversation I had with a pastor of a large evangelical church in an affluent Portland suburb illustrates this point. Knowing of my passion for social justice, this pastor informed me that several women in his church had been ministering to women in Portland's inner city. Encouraged by the fact that there were people at his church who had a vision for ministry outside the suburban context of their church walls, I nonetheless asked him how the inner-city women had ministered to his congregants. His response was something like this: "Excuse me, but what would those women have to offer ours?"

This was a dear Christian man, though perhaps a bit blind at first to his own condescending mindset. Fortunately, he soon realized what he had said. I responded to his question by saying that at the very least the inner-city Christian women could help the women from his church grasp a thing or two about surviving under oppressive conditions, and about being poor in spirit yet rich toward God, as was true of the church of Smyrna (Rev. 2:9). Such an interaction might just help the suburban women guard against the danger that riches can blind people to the state of their true spiritual condition, as was the case for the church of Laodicea (Rev. 3:17-19).

One of my former students grew up in a very affluent community, but while he was in seminary he moved into an intentional Christian community in the inner city to be salt and light to those living in the neighborhood. When people would ask him why he was ministering to poor blacks in the inner city, he would respond by saying that they were the ones ministering to him. He learned from them what a caring neighborhood community can be like, which was not something he had learned from the community where he was raised.

Christians and churches should become partners in such a way that the rich take from their own poverty and give to the poor, and the poor take from their own riches and give to the rich (James 1:9-11, 2:5). Both need each other and need to work together to benefit one another. Jesus was rich; yet he became poor and needy, humbling himself so that he could exalt us and make us rich. When he was thirsty, he even requested a cup of water from a lowly Samaritan woman, who in every other way was more needy than he was. In doing so he exalted her (John 4:1-42). He has done the same for each of us: "For you know the grace of our Lord Jesus Christ, that though he was rich, yet for your sake he became poor, so that you through his poverty might become rich" (2 Cor. 8:9).

The preceding discussion on the rich being/becoming poor and the poor being/becoming rich calls to mind two questions Marva Dawn raises: "Could suburban churches partner with inner-city churches to share financial and other resources? If they do, will the rich churches know their weakness enough to receive the immense gifts of their poorer brothers and sisters?"[12] One way to overcome unidirectional ministry would be for an affluent church to take the money set aside for a short-term mission to build church walls in Mexico and use it to pay the Mexican pastor and some of his people to come and minister to the American church in question, helping to rebuild the walls of that church's heart, a heart whose arteries are clogged by "affluenza." One of my students suggested just such a short-term missions reversal to his church elders on two occasions. Both times the response was: "Who's going to house them? They can't stay here at the church. They might dirty up the building."

Although poverty is not sexy, affluence can be deadly. This gives rise to the following question: Why is it that the church in many poor countries is spreading like wildfire through evangelism and church planting, whereas in America many of our large and successful churches are spreading through *transfer growth?* The affluent churches in the United States need to be weak enough to recognize their need and receive "riches" from their own poor sister churches in order to grow.

Multidirectional redistribution signifies mutually empowering partnerships driven by love and a sense of shared need that is rooted in faith and hope in the communal and co-missional God rather than one-way empowerment driven by autonomous pride. Only when we recognize that we cannot survive without solidarity will we come together to share resources. The problem is that the white evangelical Christian community does not recognize that it is an endangered species — that it is speaking largely to itself. It has lost its voice to speak to many sectors of an increasingly secular and cynical culture. If it wishes to regain a hearing, that community must become a partner with those minority communities that have been historically victimized by the dominant church and culture and yet transformed by the victorious love of Christ. A sense of solidarity and shared need can lead to multidirectional redistribution, which will involve, among other things, mutual recognition of ordinations, pulpit exchanges, sister-church relationships, and joint evangelistic and social-justice initiatives.

12. Dawn, *Powers, Weakness, and the Tabernacling of God* (Grand Rapids: Eerdmans, 2001), p. 110.

Multidirectional redistribution among churches is an important complement to multiethnic and multiclass churches in resisting homogeneity and upward mobility.[13] In fact, there may be situations where it is in the best interest of a particular church to remain ethnically unified, at least for a time, so as to preserve its language and cultural tradition. Majority culture believers interested in raising up multiethnic and interracial churches, yet lacking sensitivity and intentionality, may undermine the very thing they rightly desire to achieve — *multi*-ethnic churches. Well-meaning dominant cultural groups within such churches, if they are not careful, can run roughshod over small and docile groups and drown out their voices in the community's life and worship. But such precautions do not excuse the dominant groups from coming together in solidarity, and in celebration of the Lord's Supper, along with other Christian bodies in the region. Intentionality is the key. Solidarity and intentionality are crucially important today in the Asian-American Christian community because many younger Asian-American Christians are leaving their parents' native-speaking fellowships and founding new churches based on the English language. These young Christians should be very intentional about maintaining a social network with those older churches. Such networking may involve ministry partnerships, including quarterly worship celebrations and annual retreats. Many who come from Asian backgrounds, yet who do not want to be associated with their Asian heritage — similar to the way others of us struggle with our current church settings or cultural backgrounds — need to ask themselves where God is calling them. Most of us do not ask this question.[14] May God's desire for and calling on our lives consume us and our personal preferences so that we pursue what we need: the whole body, not just those parts we like.

13. Curtiss Paul DeYoung, Michael O. Emerson, George Yancey, and Karen Chai Kim, *United by Faith: The Multiracial Congregation as an Answer to the Problem of Race* (Oxford: Oxford University Press, 2003); this book, which champions the emergence of multiethnic churches, is a sequel to *Divided by Faith*.

14. The Home of Christ church network in the San Francisco Bay area is asking such questions and making valiant attempts to reconcile diverse and divergent groups in the Asian-American community, including their Asian- and English-speaking congregations.

Our personal preferences and affinities often blind us to the diverse groups and the diverse needs around us. Many Christians attending churches in affluent areas argue that their surrounding social contexts are homogeneous, that one would be hard-pressed to find ethnic minorities or the poor in those communities. But they should take another look at their surroundings. One will often find, even in affluent communities, that the wealthy employ poorer people as groundskeepers, nannies, and maids. And even if the community is totally homogeneous, their churches should become partners with other churches in the greater region to obey the biblical injunction to unity and the need for the church to identify with a given metropolitan region (see 1 Cor. 12:12-31 on unity; see 1 Cor. 1:2 and 2 Cor. 2:1 on the church's identifying with its city or region).

Solidarity will also lead to accountability between churches, which will entail guarding against a church's temptation to compete with other churches for religious consumers. That accountability will go beyond mere bulletin statements encouraging prayer support for churches in the area, churches that may have lost members to them because of their superior brands of goods and services. Those who have been beneficiaries must also work to benefit those churches that have lost out to them by sending people to minister *with* them. We are all in this together, and we all need one another. We must also bear one another's burdens, for we are all responsible for one another. This leads to the second point.

Reconciliation and the Redistribution of Responsibility and Blame

Self-examination that involves reconciliation and redistribution will entail redistribution of responsibility and blame, which is based on our corporate solidarity in Adam's sin. The Lord's Supper bears witness to the fact that we are all victimizers and that Christ alone is the pure sacrificial lamb and spotless victim. Robert Jenson, in his discussion of Jonathan Edwards's *Original Sin,* says that the idea of corporate solidarity and responsibility bound up with Adam's sin offends modern sensibilities and thus is rejected. The modern anthropological doctrine rejects the notion that each person "accept responsibility for human history's total act as my act." Yet, as Jenson argues, that modern dismissal is "morally corrosive." He reasons: "If I cannot take responsibility for humankind's act, how can I take it for that of my nation? If not for my nation's act, how for that of my family?"[15]

It is ironic that many evangelical Christians claim that they are not responsible for the sins and lives of others, whether it be those monstrous forebears who enslaved blacks or committed genocide against Native-American people or those criminal forces today that enslave women to lives of prostitution and who rob the poor of their homes through enforced gentrification and "urban renewal." Taken far enough, it will undermine their patriotic concern for the nation and their veneration of the family, as Jenson's argument suggests.

Some modern individualists — evangelical or otherwise — go so far as to conceive of human significance through the lens of productivity and consumption. If human identity is construed as "I produce and consume; therefore, I am," and if "all social relations . . . can in principle be exchanged as commodities"[16] (both of which are often implicit identity claims today), what ultimately is the point of being loyal to family and nation? What is one to make of those who virtually abandon their families to climb the corporate or ecclesiastical ladder, or those corporations who abandon their countries for tax breaks and shelters overseas? As with all commodities awaiting transaction, family and nation are valuable to the extent that they serve useful purposes. Lesslie Newbigin puts it well: according to the "post-Enlightenment project," "all human activity is absorbed into labor. It becomes an unending cycle of production for the sake of consumption." In this view, "what does not enter the market is ignored." Thus the homemaker is set to the side as insignificant because her or his work does not benefit the market (while the "gambling syndicate, arms salesman and drug pusher" do).[17]

15. Robert W. Jenson, *America's Theologian: A Recommendation of Jonathan Edwards* (Oxford: Oxford University Press, 1988), p. 150.

16. Don Slater, *Consumer Culture and Modernity* (Cambridge: Polity, 1997), p. 27.

17. Lesslie Newbigin, *Foolishness to the Greeks: The Gospel and Western Culture* (Grand Rapids: Eerdmans, 1986), pp. 30-31.

The same can be said of the democratic or consumer church tradition. If the family is no longer useful, why not abandon it, or, at the very least, humor it and ignore it? What should be done with church family members when they no longer serve the GNP of our consumer-driven churches? If focusing on the family in our churches is a means toward maximizing church growth, then the family's value is ultimately utilitarian: that is, if it does not produce results, it has no value and is no longer welcome. An individualistic, consumer church focus may in some cases promote concern for individual families, at least for families that are like one's own, but what happens if the main breadwinner loses his or her job, can no longer write the big checks for the building program, and falls out of the target-audience income bracket?

The individualistic framework of much contemporary evangelicalism bears greater similarity to enlightened liberalism than it does to biblical orthodoxy, which would involve the claim that human history's "total act" is "my act." Scripture also reveals the godly likes of Daniel repenting on behalf of his people and pleading for Jerusalem's well-being (Dan. 9:1-19). Perhaps the greatest problem here is that many of us evangelicals are not even aware of how individualistic and inhumane we are.

The church must re-envision its understanding of communal identity in view of its communal and co-missional God as involving solidarity with society at large. Christ himself was all about solidarity. Though he knew no sin, he became sin on our behalf to reconcile us with God (2 Cor. 5:21a). This will entail a radical break from the dominant American individualistic mindset that keeps us separate from others. It will require that we lay down our lives and die for our enemies rather than try to take back America from them.

American Christians must take responsibility for humanity's total act of sin. For one thing, the doctrine is biblical and theologically orthodox; for another, we *are* responsible. White evangelical Americans who do not buy the original sin argument should think again. At the very least, they should see that they are responsible for their white American forebears' sin in oppressing African-Americans, because white people today benefit from the system our American forebears put in place. If we

149

are aware of this system and do nothing to dismantle it, our culpability actually increases.

Christians are also responsible for promoting beloved community in society, for caring for the oppressed. In fact, Christians are even more responsible: not only do we share in humanity's total act of depravity, but also we are called to bear witness to Christ's mighty act of reconciliation and redemption on behalf of the whole creation. Just as we died with him, we also rose with him so that we could and can become the righteousness of God (2 Cor. 5:21b). Christ makes possible a new way of being and engagement for victim and victimizer alike.

At the Last Supper, victim and victimizer (Jesus and Judas) were both present. Victim and victimizer are also present at the Lord's Supper today, and each of us is both victim and victimizer. However, the Lord's Supper is the first supper of a new era, and in light of the Resurrection, we can respond redemptively. We now belong to a different system — one of giving and receiving, not one of blaming and betraying. Each of us is responsible, but Christ does not allow us to bear our responsibility alone. We can act redemptively, for he who was guiltless, yet victimized, rose victorious and transformed the structures that victim and victimizer inhabit, making possible a new way of being in the world. Rowan Williams puts it this way:

> I am, willy-nilly, involved in "structural violence," in economic, political, religious and private systems of relationship which diminish the other (and I must repeat once more that the victim in one system is liable to be the oppressor in another: the polarity runs through each individual). Yet I find, through the resurrection gospel, that I have a choice about colluding with these systems, a possibility of belonging to another "system" in which gift rather than diminution is constitutive. I am thus equipped to understand that structural violence is not an unshakeable monolith: critical action, constructive protest, is possible. My involvement in violence is most destructive when least self-aware, and simply understanding that involvement is a crucial first step. But to understand it in the presence of the Easter Jesus is to understand that violence is not omnipotent, and that my involve-

ment in it does not rule out the possibility of transformation of my relations.[18]

We are all "willy-nilly" involved in structural violence, including race and class divisions, a point brought home forcefully by the movie *Crash*. But the gospel goes further. Not only are we all involved in intensifying and reinforcing race and class divisions, but Christ is involved in redeeming the fallen structures and our place in them, leading us forward to a new world order. Our consuming of Christ in the celebration of the Lord's Supper by faith through the Spirit means that we are consumed by Christ, which signifies union with him and all who are in him actually and potentially, victim and victimizer alike. Such solidarity or oneness is God's response to humanity's corporate solidarity in Adam's sin. Through Christ, the firstborn of all creation and the firstborn from the dead (Col. 1:15, 18), God reconciles and redeems the cosmos and creates a new humanity in which we participate by faith in him. Therefore, Christians and churches can and must view all humanity in light of humanity's true identity, and must work together and with the citizenry at large to take responsibility for fighting against ungodly consumption and oppression in the public square.

We must use our freedom in Christ to serve one another, being consumed by Christ rather than consuming one another in incessant turf battles. Galatians 5:13-15 provides the framework for us for approaching our brothers and sisters in Christ, and by extension the world at large. The ESV translation reads:

> For you were called to freedom, brothers. Only do not use your freedom as an opportunity for the flesh, but through love serve one another. For the whole law is fulfilled in one word: "You shall love your neighbor as yourself." But if you bite and devour one another, watch out that you are not consumed by one another.

18. Rowan Williams, *Resurrection: Interpreting the Easter Gospel*, rev. ed. (Cleveland: The Pilgrim Press, 2002), p. 73.

We must no longer live in light of the old world order, victimizing our fellow victims, consuming and being consumed; instead, we must remember to bear one another's burdens, especially those of the poor, as Paul himself was eager to do in his outreach to the gentiles (Gal. 2:10). Those who do not see themselves as bearing some responsibility for the plight of the poor make the poor bear even more responsibility for the ills that plague society. Too often poor communities become the locations for prisons, super highways, mental health facilities, ex-offenders' facilities, and land designated for toxic or nuclear waste. I doubt that Crawford, Texas, Martha's Vineyard, or the east side of Vancouver, Washington (where I live), will become the site of a nuclear waste dump any time soon. Often it is only when the problems plaguing inner-city America or Native-American reservations affect the affluent and powerful individuals and corporations that authorities take significant action. Crystal meth is not a problem limited to the dispossessed of the inner cities; it is a social problem that also affects affluent suburbs and successful enterprises, and it will soon be coming to a neighborhood near you, if it is not there already. What if we possessed the sensitivity to see that society's problems do affect all of us in one way or another and that we are to bear one another's burdens for the common good of all? Fortunately, some leading Christians and successful churches boycott notions that human freedom is autonomy — with all that those notions entail for isolating them from the public sphere — and see themselves as bearing some responsibility for the poor and imprisoned. The prison ministry of Rick Warren and the Saddleback Valley Community Church takes seriously the claim that the church has a role to play in society at large, including among the downtrodden. The ministry is making a significant impact on the prison system in California and has received national exposure in a *New York Times* article.[19] This is an excellent work, and it is to be enthusiastically embraced. We can model such ministry endeavors in prisons in our own communities: we can share resources with other churches that minister to those ex-offenders, who often live in lower-

19. John Leland, "Church Reaches Out to Bring Inmates into the Fold," *New York Times News Service*, July 8, 2004.

income communities; we can provide programs and personal relationships that help these people transition back into society; we can even offer our own church facilities as halfway houses for ex-offenders, allowing them to get close, even allowing them to minister to us, for we are all debtors to God's grace.

Reconciliation and the Redistribution of Resources, Talents, and Goods

Self-examination that involves reconciliation and redistribution will entail redistribution of resources, talents, and goods. We can give because Christ drank from the cup of God's wrath, poured out his life for us, and will share liberally with us at the banquet table. As Scripture says, "When he ascended on high, he led captives in his train and gave gifts to men" (Eph. 4:8). In addition to developing and promoting much-needed prison ministries, after-school educational programs, painting days for decrepit buildings, and prayer rallies for pastors and parishioners in the region, churches in affluent communities must work together with churches in downtrodden communities to foster and maintain an "incarnate" presence of healing and hope. Not only will such activities have a lasting impact as that modeling takes place, but their eyewitness accounts will reveal the devastating impact of an unmerciful, unfettered market on depressed communities. Moreover, those church communities will have an opportunity to witness and expose usury, fraud, and extortion, and to challenge the income imbalance between corporate heads and their supporting casts of workers, and the impact of that imbalance on those who fall through the cracks. We all say that we hate poverty, and many of us try to relieve the suffering of the poor. But do we hate the conditions that make people poor?

Finally, churches and other Christian organizations must help rich offenders who come into the fold in their fight against greed. They must not look the other way while holding out the offering plate, taking the money such people have made at the expense of the poor to finance their latest church building projects. While there are many wealthy believers who give wisely and sacrificially, we easily forget — as did the church to which James directed his epistle — that the rich often oppress those less fortunate (James 2:1-7).

Little is said in evangelical circles today about how the market system has an impact on the church and society as a whole, including the unfair distribution of wealth. It would almost seem as though the market is the one area of life that the fall of humanity did not have an impact on. I observed in chapter four that our evangelical forebear Jonathan Edwards spoke against the economic inequities of the market system that was emerging in his day. Pastors and teachers today must dare to preach and teach that the economics of God's kingdom is not synonymous with free-market capitalism. Though he once described himself as a capitalist of sorts, John M. Perkins has also claimed that prophetic voices must call the American church to repent of its capitulation to the free-market system, which "has made America unfairly rich and is creating massive poverty."[20] Free-market capitalism is very good at making money, but it is not very good at distributing it. Christians, on the other hand, have been called to *redistribute* our wealth, talents, and goods. While Jesus never said that we should embrace poverty, he did tell the rich young ruler to sell his possessions and give all of the proceeds to the poor (Luke 18:18-30). But it is important to point out to young Christians who are passionate about helping the poor that we cannot give to the poor if we have no resources to redistribute. We should embrace redistribution, not poverty. Following John Wesley, we should make all that we can, so that we can save all that we can, so that we can give away all that we can.[21]

Prophetic preachers must also challenge people to revamp their values, as St. John Chrysostom did in the following charge to his affluent church to live out its faith, an exhortation that is both ancient and contemporary at the same time. When neighbors who are not Christians, he said,

20. John M. Perkins, "Stoning the Prophets," *Sojourners* (Feb. 1978): 8.

21. Wesley's exact words are, "Having first gained all you can, and secondly saved all you can, then give all you can." John Wesley, "The Use of Money," in Albert C. Outler, ed., *The Works of John Wesley*, vol. 2, Sermons II, 34-70 (Nashville: Abingdon Press, 1985), p. 277.

. . . see us building ourselves fine houses, and laying out gardens and baths, and buying fields, they are not willing to believe that we are preparing for another sort of residence away from our city. . . . Hearest thou not Christ say, that He left us to be for salt and for lights in this world, in order that we may both brace up those that are melting in luxury, and enlighten them that are darkened by the care of wealth?[22]

The call to revamp our values will mean that not only nuclear families but also church families need to take another look at the way the market mentality has distorted our vision. It will mean the realization that any particular church is not successful if it succeeds and another one fails, because, though there are many churches, still they are all parts of the one great body. Perhaps one result of this would be that there would be fewer isolated church building projects and more shared ventures. Churches can say, "We don't want to steal sheep," but if they have new, state-of-the-art children's nurseries while other churches down the street or across the tracks go without them because of limited resources, the latter churches will likely lose families to their more affluent and appealing "competitors." The moral of the story is: "If you build it, they will come." At the very least, churches should consider sharing resources with poorer churches in their area so that they, too, might have state-of-the-art buildings. In keeping our resources to ourselves we settle for very little, even as God calls us to participate in something so much more profound.

Reconciliation and the Redistribution of Ownership

However, there is more to redistribution than sharing resources. The fourth point is that self-examination that involves reconciliation and redistribution will entail redistribution of ownership. Fellow Christians are equal participants in God's kingdom work. We all have a share in God's es-

---

22. St. John Chrysostom, *The Homilies of St. John Chrysostom, Archbishop of Constantinople on the Gospel of St. Matthew*, vol. 11, A Library of Fathers of the Holy Catholic Church, Anterior to the Division of the East and West (Oxford: John Henry Parker, 1843), pp. 171-72.

tate, and thus all sit at his dining table; we also have the privilege of inviting others to the banquet. As a result, churches can work together in particular areas of need; that is, affluent and poor churches can together take ownership of depressed communities. Following Perkins's lead, churches can help form "local enterprises that meet local needs and employ indigenous people."[23] This will involve giving the poor the capital they need (and cannot get due to recurring redlining) to take ownership of property and keep the money in the community. Churches can also become partners together to foster ownership of businesses among the local people. Such actions will mean giving wealthy individuals the opportunity to invest in something of greater value than the stock market. For as Jesus said, whatever you do for the least of his brothers, you do it for him (Matt. 25:40).

It is not enough to give hungry people fish to eat; nor is it enough to teach them how to fish. Perkins says that the "give people a fish and they'll eat for a day" line was the motto of 1960s community development, and "teach people to fish and they'll eat for a lifetime" was the 1970s model. Though the latter is a marked improvement on the former, neither one goes far enough to meet the "enormous challenges of the urban poor today." For Perkins, the approach needed today involves asking the question, "Who owns the pond?" He goes on to say: "The fact that young men felt no remorse for torching businesses in their own community during the Los Angeles riots indicates how little was at stake in their eyes. I imagine they would have felt differently if these businesses had been owned by neighbors, family members, and friends" (Perkins, p. 119).

Ownership is not simply a matter of owning the title; it is also about ensuring that the poor with whom we become partners in rebuilding communities have a sense of accomplishment. We can accomplish many things in life if we don't care who gets the credit. The key to explosive and long-term community-development vitality is to ensure that the people in a depressed community fully believe that they are responsible for repairing the foundations and walls of their community. Perkins gets at this idea when he quotes a Chinese poem:

23. John M. Perkins, *Beyond Charity: The Call to Christian Community Development* (Grand Rapids: Baker Books, 1993), p. 120.

Go to the people
Live among them
Learn from them
Love them
Start with what they know
Build on what they have:
But of the best leaders
When their task is done
The people will remark
"We have done it ourselves."[24]

Evangelical Christians should be redistributing their resources and sharing responsibility for the well-being of the church and its surrounding community. This will entail helping the poor of their community take ownership of the pond in view of the communal and co-missional God, who owns everything — including the pond — and who shares ownership, authority, control, honor, and power with his people (Matt. 10:1, 28:18-20). Jesus made the twelve disciples apostles, and he gave them authority over the fallen powers and humanity's fallen condition (Matt. 10:1-2). Genesis 1 tells us that God shares his dominion with all humanity (Gen. 1:28).

Evangelicals should not limit their partnerships or redistribution efforts to evangelical church networks — or even to Christians, for that matter. They should see their church walls as permeable not only to fellow evangelical believers but also to the broader church and world. For if God has given authority to political powers to rule (Rom. 13:1-7), evangelicals can work with these powers and other groups to bring God's bounty to all.[25] One reason why evangelical churches and institutions

---

24. Chinese poem as quoted in John M. Perkins, "What Is Christian Community Development?" in John M. Perkins, *Restoring At-Risk Communities: Doing It Together and Doing It Right* (Grand Rapids: Baker Books, 1995), p. 18.

25. An excellent example of this work is Mission Solano in Fairfield, California, founded and directed by Ron Marlette, an evangelical Christian. Mission Solano has become partners with evangelicals, mainline Protestants, adherents of other religions, secularists, business leaders, and officials of city, county, and state to provide holistic

should work with other Christian churches is that evangelicals have a great deal to offer in "their vitality, their zeal for evangelism, and their commitment to Scripture," according to the authors of the Princeton Proposal for Christian Unity. The statement goes on to say that evangelicals "demonstrate a spirit of cooperation with each other and sometimes with others that breaks down old barriers, creates fellowship among formerly estranged Christians, and anticipates further unity. The free-church ecclesiologies of some evangelicals bring a distinct vision of unity to the ecumenical task."[26]

Evangelicals do not exhaust the membership of the church universal, and they would do well to heed the following recommendations of the Princeton Proposal: they should "accept invitations to participate" in ecumenical discussions, "discern and celebrate living faith beyond their boundaries," "practice hospitality and pursue catholicity" (as in unity with the whole church), and use "their resources" not only to benefit their own causes and concerns but also to "work for the health of all Christian communities" (p. 56).

Evangelical churches and organizations should also partner with non-Christian groups in situations where there is common ground. This has historical precedent. Though Jonathan Edwards spoke emphatically of regeneration's importance for effecting optimal benefit in social action, he nonetheless encouraged his followers to become partners with non-Christians "for the sake of common moral objectives."[27] Carl F. H. Henry also spoke of the importance of regeneration for producing lasting fruit in the area of social activism; but he also encouraged evangelical Christians to cooperate with non-Christians toward moral goals they

---

care and support for the homeless, including nomadic sheltering. For more information on Mission Solano, see www.missionsolano.org. Another institution doing significant work in this arena is the newly organized Oregon Center for Christian Values (www.occv.org).

26. Carl E. Braaten and Robert W. Jenson, ed., *In One Body through the Cross: The Princeton Proposal for Christian Unity* (Grand Rapids: Eerdmans, 2003), pp. 55-56.

27. Gerald R. McDermott, *One Holy and Happy Society: The Public Theology of Jonathan Edwards* (University Park: The Pennsylvania State University Press, 1992), pp. 180-81.

held in common.[28] Such common-ground initiatives must go beyond matters that pertain to individual morality.

The church can only serve the world if the church holds firmly to the politics of Jesus. At times, though, the church will find that the world will call it to account, holding it to the political values of Jesus' "upside-down" kingdom, whether or not they are truly cognizant of that kingdom's claims and aims. Just as churches can learn from one another, they can also benefit from partnerships with "the world," because the boundary between them is permeable.[29] For *all* people are created in the image of the triune God (Gen. 1:26-27).

Reconciliation and redistribution of ownership will mean that churches working together and with the larger society will emphasize common qualities and shared values, but they should do so without abandoning their distinctive qualities and traits, all of which can bring richness to church and civil unity. Those qualities should not divide churches or separate the church from society. Christians and churches should glory in what they have in common with one another and with the world in these ventures — more than preoccupying themselves with what separates them.[30] Concerning the church, mutual union with Christ through the Spirit nurtured by Scripture and the Lord's Supper should be at the center of all interchurch discussions.

Scripture teaches that there is one body, one Spirit, one Lord, one faith, one baptism covering Jew and Greek, slave and free, one God over

28. Carl F. H. Henry, *The Uneasy Conscience of Modern Fundamentalism* (Grand Rapids: Eerdmans, 1947; reprint, with foreword by Richard J. Mouw, 2003), p. 79. Ray Bakke points out that in 1893, R. A. Torrey, the president of Moody Bible Institute (a leading dispensationalist school), served on Chicago's Slum Clearance Committee. The person chairing the committee was a leading Unitarian clergyman. According to Bakke, it was only after 1920 that the Bible institute movement pulled away from public and social engagement. See Ray Bakke, *A Theology as Big as the City* (Downers Grove, IL: InterVarsity Press, 1997), pp. 161-62.

29. Stanley Hauerwas claims that the "boundary" between the church and world is "permeable" and that "something has gone wrong when the church is not learning from the world how to live faithfully to God." Hauerwas, *Performing the Faith: Bonhoeffer and the Practice of Nonviolence* (Grand Rapids: Brazos Press, 2004), pp. 231-32.

30. Braaten and Jenson, eds., *In One Body through the Cross*, p. 34.

all, one Spirit to drink, one loaf to consume (1 Cor. 10:17; 12:12-14; Eph. 4:4-6). Concerning the loaf, Paul says, "We, who are many, are one body, for we all partake of the one loaf" (1 Cor. 10:17). In addition to the Lord's Supper, it is vitally important to emphasize unity in the Word of truth: "However loudly our rhetoric insists that Christian discipleship is not a matter of consumer choice, the point will be made effectively only when potential believers encounter all around them Christian communities united in shared disciplines of faithfulness to the apostolic word" (Braaten and Jenson, p. 42). Scripture is potent and must serve as a key basis for pursuing ecumenical solidarity. While doctrine may at times divide, commitment to Scripture's storied and Christocentric truth will set people free: it will bring unity where there were divisions, and it will give them a heart for civic involvement, especially in terms of fighting against ongoing racial tensions and poverty.

Reconciliation and redistribution of ownership will entail that a profound sense of calling and vocation must replace undue preoccupation with personal preferences and affinities. Church leaders must challenge their people to reflect on their sense of calling to their particular church, to the church at large, to the region, and to the world. These leaders must train people to go deep in discernment, focusing on the values of God's heart and God's call as Lord of their lives.

Reconciliation and the Redistribution of Glory

Fifth, self-examination that involves reconciliation and redistribution will entail redistribution of glory, in this case giving it not to ourselves but to God. As Psalm 115:1 declares, "Not to us, O LORD, not to us, but to your name be the glory because of your love and faithfulness." The Giver of gifts, talents, and resources must take precedence over the gifted, who in turn are to offer up their treasures to the Lord. Marva Dawn says:

> Why is it that so many people can talk freely about how great their church is, but find it much more difficult to converse with others about the greatness of their Lord? "Charismatic" pastors, "thrilling"

worship leaders, "dynamic" musicians, or "exciting" worship services frequently become what is worshiped instead.[31]

One finds here a close parallel to Paul's struggle in Corinth, where some were saying, "I follow Paul," and others, "I follow Apollos," and still others, "I follow Cephas" (1 Cor. 1:12); still others aligned themselves with the super-apostles (2 Cor. 11–12). Paul's response to these divisions (1 Cor. 3) was apt then and is apt now: "What then is Apollos? What is Paul? Servants through whom you believed, as the Lord assigned to each. I planted, Apollos watered, but God gave the growth. So neither he who plants nor he who waters is anything, but only God who gives the growth" (1 Cor. 3:5-7, ESV).

This passage of Scripture must come to dominate the church's imagination and its discussions of church growth. It is not about you or me; nor is it about this or that church. In fact, it is not even, in the end, about the church of the city. It is about the Lord. Christ's all-consuming glory captured Paul's imagination, and it led Paul to seek cooperation between Christians in a given church and among churches. We can share with one another because God shares his glory with Christ, and Christ, as the incarnate agent of the communal and co-missional God in the world, shares it with us. As John 17:22 makes clear, "I have given them the glory you gave me, that they may be one as we are one."

Jesus became poor and took our sin so that we might become truly rich and righteous, receive his gifts and authority, and share in his glory. He did this freely, graciously, with no compulsion. For the beloved communal joy set before him — communion with us as partakers in the life of the communal and co-missional God — Jesus endured the cross, despising its shame (Heb. 12:2; 2 Pet. 1:4). Scripture and the Lord's Supper bear witness to the fact that Jesus gave up less for more. And this same Scripture and Supper invite us to give up less to gain more: the divine-human beloved community, a community of cooperation, not compulsion. The all-consuming vision of Christ has inspired great awakenings through the ages. May it also inspire them in our day.

31. Dawn, *Powers, Weakness, and the Tabernacling of God,* p. 108.

An All-Consuming Vision of Cooperation

Edwards's words in *The Great Awakening* tie together the ideas of being consumed by Christ and cooperating on behalf of Christ. The heads of Israel's tribes contributed their wealth to build the tabernacle in Exodus 35:21-29: "These are the days of erecting the tabernacle of God amongst us." Just as the goldsmiths and merchants rebuilt Jerusalem's wall (Neh. 3:22), so the days are "not very far off, when the sons of Zion shall come from far, bringing their silver and their gold with them" to God and the "Holy One of Israel,"

> ... when the merchants of the earth shall trade for Christ more than for themselves, and their merchandise and hire shall be holiness to the Lord, and shall not be treasured or laid up for posterity, but shall be for them that dwell before the Lord, to eat sufficiently, and for durable clothing; and when the ships of Tarshish shall bring the wealth of the distant parts of the earth, to the place of God's sanctuary, and to make the place of his feet glorious.... The days are coming, when the great and rich men of the world shall bring their honor and glory into the church, and shall as it were strip themselves, to spread their garments under Christ's feet, as he enters triumphantly into Jerusalem....[32]

Will the merchants of the various churches rise up in solidarity to overcome the market forces, to contribute their wealth to build the tabernacle? Will the sons of Zion take out the Ark and rebuild the city wall, and will the merchants trade more for the selfless Christ than for themselves and thus welcome Christ in as he turns Nineveh and Babylon into the New Jerusalem? I pray that these days are "not very far off." Only when the churches in a given region unite as one church in love around the Ark by the Spirit of true revival, even becoming partners with those outside the church to contend for the same moral objectives, will God's people begin to become now what they are destined to be in God's fu-

32. Jonathan Edwards, *The Great Awakening*, ed. C. C. Goen (New Haven: Yale University Press, 1972), pp. 514-15.

ture — the beloved community, a city on a hill, whose light illumines the world,[33] where the kings and nations bring their splendor and glory into the church.

That day will dawn only when churches and their leaders consume Christ and are consumed by Christ. Only then will they cooperate with one another to take captive the market forces and relocate, reconcile, and redistribute their wealth for the sake of Christ in the church universal, and beyond its walls, bearing witness to a nobler vision.

33. Jonathan Edwards, "Peaceable and Faithful Amid Division and Strife," in M. X. Lesser, ed., *Sermons and Discourses, 1734-1738*, vol. 19, *The Works of Jonathan Edwards* (New Haven: Yale University Press, 1972), p. 674.

A Nobler Vision of Patchwork Quilts and Church Potlucks

It is not simply what we say that matters, but also what we communicate. The *Willamette Week* article on evangelical Christianity that I referred to in the introduction suggested that, to many people, evangelicalism communicates a patchwork quilt with an overall embroidered pattern of a sappy, overstylized, surreal-looking Jesus. His saccharine smile and outstretched hand convey shallowness, perhaps even shrouding less-than-pleasant motives. Reading between the lines, one can see the unsettling image emerge of a Jesus who on the one hand entertains warlike ambitions and on the other hand pursues the American dream of life, liberty, leisure, and happiness. What images of Jesus and his kingdom do we wish to construct and convey?

I participated in a dialogue at a Buddhist temple not long ago. A Buddhist priest friend of mine had invited me to speak to members of his temple community about evangelical Christianity. The event was part of a larger effort he and I have undertaken to promote dialogue and understanding between those on the sociopolitical left and right in order to defuse the harsh rhetoric of the culture wars and create understanding.[1] Many in his community feel threatened by evangelical Christianity. The threat, real or perceived, is of a Religious Right seeking to

---

1. This ongoing dialogue and partnership is chronicled in Sallie Jiko Tisdale, "Beloved Community," in *Tricycle: The Buddhist Review* (Fall 2006): 54-59, 114-15 (with accompanying sidebars).

take back America — and succeeding. The role evangelicals were assumed to have had in helping re-elect George W. Bush to a second term in office in 2004, accompanied by the victory of an amendment banning gay marriage in Oregon, was evidence enough for many in that community that the Religious Right had already taken back America. So the news in the Zen temple that an evangelical Christian leader was coming to speak to them naturally evoked anger and fear among many. Indeed, not only do the Left and Right resent each other; each side also fears the other, fears that neither side seems willing to examine.

During the course of defining evangelicalism, I talked about the fundamentalist-modernist controversy, and I addressed ways to build bridges between those from the opposing camps. I also related two stories that convey a nobler vision of the evangelical movement than the one often perceived or experienced by those outside it. The first was the story about John M. Perkins sharing his testimony at Reed College, which I told in the introduction. The other elaborates on Donald Miller's discussion of the confession booth event at Reed College's festival, Ren Fayre, in his book *Blue Like Jazz*. Ren Fayre is an annual event at the college when, as Miller says, "they shut down the campus so students can party."[2] Don, Tony the Beat Poet, and others built a confession booth so that people could make confessions during this party-hard weekend. A Portland-area conservative talk-radio host similar to Rush Limbaugh found out that Don, Tony, and others — all evangelical Christians — were preparing something big at Reed College, and he mistakenly assumed that they were going to give those liberal Reedies the business, taking the culture war rhetoric and hostility to a new level. But in speaking with Tony, the radio host soon came to realize that there was no story here, at least not the kind he wanted to broadcast on his program.

Tony, Don, and the others went the whole way with the booth: it was as though they had been transported in time from the Middle Ages, wearing monks' robes and ringing cowbells. One of the student revelers who entered the booth thought the whole thing was a big joke. As he

2. Donald Miller, *Blue Like Jazz: Nonreligious Thoughts on Christian Spirituality* (Nashville: Thomas Nelson Publishers, 2003), p. 116.

was making fun of it, Tony said to him, "This is a confession booth, and I would like to begin. As a Christian, I want to ask your forgiveness for all those times when my fellow Christians judged you and condemned you. . . ." After Tony stopped speaking of the brokenness of his Christian faith, the young man, sitting just inches away from him in the tiny booth, replied, "That is the f-ing most beautiful thing I have ever heard." He then began to express to Tony — really sharing with him — the brokenness of his own life.

When I finished my talk that evening at the Zen temple, one of the Buddhist lay monks said, "If anyone has a corner on compassion, it should be you guys with your belief that God came down to earth and became one of us, to identify with us in our brokenness. What happened?" The vision of Christianity of John M. Perkins and Tony the Beat Poet spoke to those gathered there, shedding light on the compassion sitting in Christianity's corner. How I long for compassion to come out of that dark corner and into the center of evangelical Christianity's engagement of the broader culture, to have an impact on individual personal relationships and to deconstruct the structures that divide us.

The vision of evangelical Christianity expressed by Perkins and Tony rarely gets communicated to the press. But then, why should it? It does not dominate the evangelical imagination. What is required is a nobler vision of the faith and of what its patchwork quilt should look like, an image Randall Balmer uses in his conclusion to *Mine Eyes Have Seen the Glory*, a book that takes the reader on a journey through evangelicalism's "unwieldy" subculture, which he compares to a patchwork quilt:

> A quilt, especially one produced at a quilting bee, is folk art rather than fine art; it requires the work of many hands, each of which contributes its own "signature" to the project. Its beauty, moreover, lies precisely in its variegated texture and even, sometimes, in the absence of an overall pattern. Unlike a mosaic, it is also quintessentially American.[3]

3. Balmer, *Mine Eyes Have Seen the Glory: A Journey into the Evangelical Subculture in America* (New York: Oxford University Press, 1993), pp. 279-80.

One of the patches on the quilt that Balmer surveys is John M. Perkins's life and ministry. Balmer says that Perkins's Voice of Calvary in Mississippi "represents a nobler vision, to be sure — one of racial harmony and social justice — but it is no less illusory, no less incongruous with the larger world" (Balmer, p. 282). It is indeed illusory if one defines reality in terms of its proximity to the dominant culture, evangelical or otherwise. But if one defines reality in terms of the beloved community disclosed in Scripture's eschatological vision of the messianic banquet, then Perkins's nobler vision is real. My hope is that the Perkins vision of beloved community will capture more and more the imagination of the evangelical church across this land, reconfiguring its patchwork quilt pattern of Jesus.

People actualize a vision. If you had an opportunity to cast a vision of what evangelical Christianity's patchwork quilt patterned after Jesus' likeness should look like, what would it be? How would that *Willamette Week* article read ten years after the fact? I am not suggesting here that everyone should do exactly what Perkins does; uniformity would take away from the beauty of the patchwork's diversity. Rather, I am hoping that the overall pattern would convey a more compassionate-looking Jesus, a servant whose outstretched arm bears a towel, a mediator who seeks after racial harmony and social justice.

Such a Perkinsonian quilt for the evangelical church that I envision would bear patches of inner-city soup kitchens and thrift shops, of Willow Creek–like car shops where mechanics volunteer their time to fix up donated cars for those who cannot afford cars. The quilt would also bear patches of medical clinics such as the one at New Heights Church in Vancouver, Washington, where doctors and nurses give free medical care to those without health insurance. Budding church partnerships in a given region would dot the patchwork landscape, where megachurches share their abundant resources with impoverished faith communities and receive from the latter their abundant life in Christ. Not only will these affluent churches receive their reward in heaven for ministering to the least of Jesus' brethren (Luke 14:12-14); they will come to realize, as Jesus also notes, that the least of these are often the greatest of these (Rev. 2:9). There would also be a patch for Pastor John, who turned down an offer to join the staff of a megachurch in order to try to turn a dysfunctional church in rural Oregon around, while also becoming partners with an African-American pastor from Portland to build bridges between whites and blacks. There would no doubt be a patch for those churches who take on board the purposeful work of Rick Warren and the Saddleback Valley Community Church in the California state penitentiary system, another for those backing Warren's partnership with Bruce Wilkinson (of *Prayer of Jabez* fame) to fight against poverty and AIDS in Africa while offering support to those with AIDS closer to home,[4] and still another for those who show love to gays and lesbians by shielding them from hate crimes. A patch would be reserved for the Advent Conspiracy, which Rick McKinley of Imago Dei Community in Portland masterminded with fellow pastors across the land. At Christmas they worship Jesus by resisting "Herod's" empire of greed by giving relationally, taking money otherwise spent on stuff to build wells for clean drinking water in impoverished places around the world. Northwest Medical Teams, along with Prison Fellowship's and World Vision's area chapters, would have their own patches, as would Shepherd's Door, a ministry to battered women, and My Father's House, a Christian outreach that provides temporary shelter for homeless families and helps them get back on their feet.

Ministries such as these are out there working in the American culture and in the world, but they do not dominate the theological, ecclesiastical, or popular evangelical imagination. Nor do many of them touch us where we live our personal lives, because all too often we keep them at arm's length as projects that our churches sponsor. Instead, we need to develop church membership roles, partnerships, and internships where we can internalize relationships with those on society's fringe rather than dehumanizing or demonizing the "other." Only when our

4. See Timothy C. Morgan, "Mr. Jabez Goes to Africa: Bruce Wilkinson Expands His Borders to Include Racial Reconciliation and HIV/AIDS," *Christianity Today*, November 2003, pp. 45-50; see also Timothy C. Morgan, "Purpose Driven in Rwanda," *Christianity Today*, October 2005, pp. 32-36, 90-91. REACH Ministries is one such labor of love here in the United States that ministers to children with AIDS and their families (see www.reachministries.org).

outreach programs reach *us* for Christ will the kingdom of God dawn in our midst. Thus it is vital that the quilt have patches bearing the likenesses of the rich and poor, blacks and whites, the healthy and diseased, all worshiping, working, and "wining and dining" together at God's agape feast.

As beautiful as this image of a patchwork quilt with its Perkinsonian portrayal of Jesus may be, the fear of scarcity will keep such a vision from being realized. "There is not enough to go around!" we fear. This fear reveals an anxiety disorder that stems from our not eating and drinking our fill from the eschatological banquet in the here and now (see Isa. 25, Luke 12 and 14, Rev. 19). We settle for less, far less; indeed, we settle for base consumerism rather than being consumed by Christ and his bountiful future feast in the present tense, wherein we can experience true life, true liberty, and the true pursuit of joyful happiness. There is a nagging sense in each of our souls and imaginations that there could be more, much more. Many, if not all, of us can relate to U2's Bono when he sings, "I still haven't found what I'm looking for."[5] Christ's perfect love celebrated at his agape feast is alone sufficient to cast out such fear, and to stem the spread of apathy and anger among those who are burned out by waging war on the fallen powers, who go forth driven by guilt, not by God's grace. What we need is a vision of a potluck table on which the patchwork quilt is spread, where everyone brings a dish for all to share, where bread is broken, the grapevine's nectar poured, and where Jesus is found serving those worn down and despairing from the heat of the battle.

Here we might think of Luke 12, where Jesus speaks of the rich fool, of the fear of scarcity, and of his own return from a banquet to serve his servants who stayed up late waiting for him. Jesus will usher his servants into the great banqueting hall for the feast, which the Father has prepared for him and for his guests. Seated at the table, I envision Jerry Falwell and Tim LaHaye next to Bono, and Stanley Hauerwas beside James Dobson — the lamb next to the lion, as it were (though we can no

---

5. The song by this title appears on U2's album *The Joshua Tree*. "I Still Haven't Found What I'm Looking For," *The Joshua Tree* (cp1987 U2).

longer tell who is the lamb and who the lion). Though I have scarcely mentioned them in this book, they were between the lines on many pages.

Indeed, we will be surprised at some of the odd couples we did not expect to see sitting at the same table there. But even in our own culture today we can see surprising partnerships forming. In a *Rolling Stone* interview, Bono discusses his surprising work with those from the political and religious Right Wing, such as Jesse Helms, in addressing global problems like the AIDS epidemic. In expressing his view of the American evangelical movement, Bono says:

> I'm wary of faith outside of actions. I'm wary of religiosity that ig-
> nores the wider world. In 2001, only seven percent of evangelicals
> polled felt it incumbent upon themselves to respond to the AIDS
> emergency. This appalled me. I asked for meetings with as many
> church leaders as would have them with me. I used my background in
> the Scriptures to speak to them about the so-called leprosy of our age
> and how I felt Christ would respond to it. And they had better get to it
> quickly, or they would be very much on the other side of what God
> was doing in the world. Amazingly, they did respond. I couldn't be-
> lieve it. It almost ruined it for me — 'cause I love giving out about the
> church and Christianity. But they actually came through: Jesse Helms,
> you know, publicly repents for the way he thinks about AIDS. I've
> started to see this community as a real resource in America. I have de-
> scribed them as "narrow-minded idealists." If you can widen the aper-
> ture of that idealism, these people want to change the world. They
> want their lives to have meaning. And it's one of the things that the
> Democratic Party has missed out on. You know, so much of the moral
> high ground in the past was Democratic: FDR, RFK, Cesar Chavez.
> Now I suppose it's Hillary's passion for cheaper medical care. And
> Teddy Kennedy, of course.[6]

6. Jann S. Wenner, "Bono: The Rolling Stone Interview," *Rolling Stone*, Nov. 3, 2005. I have excerpted this portion of the interview from the website: Jann S. Wenner, *Rolling Stone: Bono* (excerpted from RS 986, Nov. 3, 2005, http://www.rollingstone.com/news/ story/8651280/bono (Oct. 20, 2006).

Pastor John will be at the great banquet hall as well, right between Rick Warren and Bill Hybels, and down a ways from Marva Dawn, William Wilberforce, Mother Teresa, Richard Cizik of the NAE, Dorothy Day, and Suzie Slonaker of REACH Ministries. The homeless man who died of AIDS while sharing the Good News of God's love and hope in Christ with others on the street will be seated with Billy Graham and a host of ordinary radicals caught up in Christ's irresistible revolution.[7] Jim Wallis and Walter Rauschenbusch will be sitting right across from Dwight Moody, some migrant workers, and a few modern-day Mary Magdalenes and "tax collectors." America's theologians, Jonathan Edwards and Martin Luther King, Jr., will also be there, talking with Pat Robertson, John M. Perkins, John Paul II, Maximus the Confessor, and Oscar Romero, while the King of Kings will be lavishing his love on each one of them, beginning with the least.

There will be no need for assigned seating, and though *everyone* is invited to the banquet, there will be enough room for all. There will be no need for the rich fool to build bigger and bigger storehouses, nor for people to worry about having enough for tomorrow. For God in Christ, who is all-sufficient, will fill our lives with divine delights. The Spirit and the Bride will invite all of us to come and drink from the river of life without price and to eat and drink from the table to our hearts' content. Let us pray for that day's coming, and looking toward it, let us be as holy fools, giving and receiving from Christ and one another again and again.

In the end, the ultimate vision is that of the triune God's action in the world, a God who has the corner on compassion in engaging people's lives and the structures they inhabit. This God is all-consuming holy love, who spreads that love abroad in our hearts and the world, and who invites us to the marriage feast, opening wide the gates and blowing the doors off booths of private confession so that we all can come to him directly, corporately, publicly — and truly have a party. Neither Christian

---

7. See Shane Claiborne, *The Irresistible Revolution: Living as an Ordinary Radical* (Grand Rapids: Zondervan Publishing Company, 2006); see also Rob Moll, "The New Monasticism," *Christianity Today*, Sept. 2005, pp. 38-46, an essay on Claiborne and the emergence of ordinary though radical monastic communities in depressed urban settings.

practice nor an imaginative theological icon — nor even a renewed passion for social justice — will sustain God's people. It is God alone who can sustain us, coming to us through the indwelling and empowering Word and the Holy Spirit, the God who enlivens our practices, inspires our imaginations, and gives us hope to pursue beloved community in our own day. This community sees no divisions between race and class, between black and white and Asian-American and Native American, between rich and poor, between healthy and diseased, between young and old. Meeting us in our time of need as we stand firm in the struggle against the fallen powers of base consumerism in the church and beyond, this God will be with us always, even to the end of the age, and beyond it to the eternal dawning of the new age. Consumed by this vision, I raise my glass to offer a toast to Christ and to you, and to that day when we celebrate together at the everlasting party.

> Come, my Way, my Truth, my Life:
> Such a Way, as gives us breath:
> Such a Truth, as ends all strife:
> And such a Life, as killeth death.
>
> Come, my Light, my Feast, my Strength:
> Such a Light, as shows a feast:
> Such a Feast, as mends in length:
> Such a Strength, as makes his guest.
>
> Come, my Joy, my Love, my Heart:
> Such a Joy, as none can move:
> Such a Love, as none can part:
> Such a Heart, as joyes in love.[8]

---

8. George Herbert, "The Call," in *The Poetical Works of George Herbert* (New York: D. Appleton and Co., 1857), p. 199.

Afterword

Consuming Jesus is a powerful book. But it is more than a book. It has the potential to serve as a catalyst for a movement whereby the evangelical community repents of its consumerist heart and practices and responds to God's all-consuming love to tackle the pressing race and class problems in the church and broader culture today. It has been a long time coming.

As an African American evangelical from the state of Mississippi who took part in the Civil Rights movement, I experienced firsthand the horrors of racial discrimination and poverty. Over the years, I have painfully pondered why so few of my white evangelical brothers and sisters joined us at that time in protesting the injustices committed against minorities and the poor in this country by proclaiming in word and deed "justice for all." Racial discrimination and oppression of the poor still persist in this country; the evangelical community's same supposed indifference toward race and class divisions has also persisted through the years up until the present time.

Evangelicalism had been at the forefront of the abolition of slavery in this country and in England. And the Bible which we evangelicals hold in such high regard places a high premium on the importance of ministering to the poor, the foreigner, and the orphan and widow in their distress. Why is it so difficult for us to see?

Consuming Jesus helps us see why it is we evangelicals often don't see the race and class problems before our eyes in our churches and society. Dr. Paul Louis Metzger has provided a masterful overview of the formative years of the fundamentalist-evangelical church, and how certain historical forces and contemporary trends have led to the fundamental loss of an integral connection between faith and works and a redemptive prophetic voice and prophetic people within evangelicalism today. His redemptive theological paradigm for engagement and inspirational vision of the future can help prepare the evangelical community to be truly a missional movement of God's Spirit consumed by Jesus—not consumerism.

Consuming Jesus can serve as a key resource for discipling the emerging generation to deal with the pressing race and class divisions in our day as God's witnessing and prophetic people, providing an answer to the question: "How can we act justly and love mercy and walk humbly with our God?" As someone who has given his life to community development rooted in the biblical principles of relocation, reconciliation, and redistribution, I want to continue to participate in the answer to that question and to the building of that missional and prophetic paradigm. So, in what follows, I am going to share with you some of my own thoughts as to how we can take this book and make it part of a movement of God's Spirit in the communities in which we live.

The breakdown of the family, the commuter church, and the prosperity gospel erode the foundations of our society. The split-apart family, the back-and-forth commuter church, and the leave-the-poor-behind prosperity gospel success story do nothing to stem the poverty, crime, and violence that we see played out on the evening news. In contrast, families who stay together, churches that maintain a vital presence in a community, and those who abandon their upwardly mobile ways to identify with others less fortunate than they are preserve society and guard against the deterioration of local communities across America. The evangelical church has to recreate family and community by becoming an incarnate presence in society rather than remaining transient and self-consumed, by proclaiming the gospel of reconciliation rather than the gospel reduced to church growth and success. If we truly incarnate the church in a community, then we are better able to participate in God's redemption of the poor from oppression and act out divine jubilee justice.

All too often, we think of the church simply as a building with pro-grams aimed at making sure the church survives and thrives. On this model, people do everything possible to keep the show going. This view of the church is not missional. And as far as the poor in the surrounding community are concerned, they are viewed simply as a side issue—sim-ply the beneficiaries of our charity. In some cases, we may actually go so far as to invite these beneficiaries of our charity to church. But charity does not build community. It fosters dependence on the one hand and separation on the other hand—keeping the poor at the far end of our outstretched hand.

In our society today, the rich are getting so rich that they cannot af-ford to help the poor. The nation itself cannot afford to help the poor. In-stead, America gives the poor charity. Christ's church must set the ex-ample by identifying with Christ and identify with the poor in love, not charity. Christ went so far as to become poor so that we might become the riches of God. As his community, we must move to the place of see-ing the church as an extension of Christ's missional presence in the com-munity, where justice for the poor is central. Christ followers must go to the poor, not primarily for the purpose of inviting the poor to church, but *to be the church* in their midst. John Wesley made the poor central to every aspect of his ministry. So in evangelism, he went out to where the poor were—such as in the fields and mines. He also encouraged people to make and save as much as they could so as to give as much as they could to the poor. Wesley taught and lived out a theology of justice. The response to his methods among the people of his day was overwhelm-ing. Like Wesley, we are to be the people of divine justice who love peo-ple into our community by reaching out holistically to them with the good news in word and deed!

We are attempting to build community where we live right here in Mississippi. Recent reports have stated that four out of ten Mississippi residents live in poverty, and that probably half of that four out of ten live in what some sociologists call extreme poverty. I have also read that the state of Mississippi has the third highest incarceration rate in the na-tion behind Louisiana, which is first, and Texas, which is second. We have begun a work here in Jackson, Mississippi, called the Zechariah 8

Community Project, which my daughter Elizabeth envisioned. Zechariah 8 grew out of her experience of working with youth over many years where she witnessed firsthand the negative impact the breakdown of family and community can have on children's lives. Elizabeth came to the conclusion that these youth needed a family environment similar to what is described in Zechariah 8, where the values, culture, and heritage of the old could be transferred to the young.

The Zechariah 8 Community is in the heart of an inner-city community that shows all the signs that it could become one of the worst crime areas in the nation. Such communities in disrepair bear witness to a growing nationwide epidemic. If you were to ask her what makes her think we are facing an "epidemic" nationally, Elizabeth would tell you that 70 percent of the nation's African American children are born out-of-wedlock. The 2000 Census reported that the urban community is 88 percent black, and that it has the highest abortion rate of any group in the U.S. The National Fatherhood Initiative based in Gaithersburg, Maryland, reports that 60 percent of rapists, 72 percent of adolescent murderers, and 70 percent of long-term prison inmates come from fatherless homes. We have found that the best way for the church to participate with God in fighting the spread of this epidemic is to engage in the community development work of relocation—living incarnationally and intentionally in communities of need, reconciliation—restoring relationships with God and neighbor, and redistribution—sharing gifts, resources, abilities, talents, and our very own lives with people.

As much good as the Christian Community Development Association that I founded has done in the past and present, we have to move forward and develop some new models for engagement. We must go to our colleges, universities, and seminaries and find able and passionate people who will partner with those of us who are doing the work on the streets, returning to the Bible in search of fresh ideas and relevant practices—like new wine that is poured out into new wineskins. We have to do some new thinking from the ground up in order to do what's needed for the up-and-coming generation. Our evangelical colleges, universities, and seminaries need to assist local churches by training a new type of church leader to do this.

I have found Dr. Metzger's adaptation and application of my paradigm of relocation, reconciliation, and redistribution in his book to be quite inspiring. Redistribution works on many levels and in a variety of ways. New partnerships must form; for strength is found in solidarity with others. For example, as a practitioner, I can lend credibility and vitality to my brother Paul's work, just as his particular work as a theologian engaging culture provides much needed foundations for our own community development work to take deeper root and flourish. He and I are beginning a partnership through the John M. Perkins Foundation and The Institute for the Theology of Culture: New Wine, New Wineskins of Multnomah Biblical Seminary that we would love to extend to you. We need your help. Will you please join us? We long for the Zechariah 8 dream that we have been living out here in Jackson, Mississippi, to be fulfilled. We have only just begun to build that community. We also long to see Zechariah-like works rise up from the ashes in dispossessed communities all around the country. Moreover, we desire to see new wine flowing out of new wineskins across the land. As Paul says in this book, we the church must get beyond our special interests, turf battles, and individualism and consumerism and work together as his people—consumed by Jesus—so as to consume race and class divisions inside the church and beyond. But churches cannot do it alone.

My hope is that schools like Multnomah Bible College, Multnomah Biblical Seminary, and other colleges, universities, and seminaries would partner with us and take on the challenge of training young folks to go out and do community development work in depressed communities across America. With this in mind, we will also need to think strategically about the economics that would undergird such missional endeavors. We have to train the young people so well that they would go out and do the work, not in the old-fashioned way of going out to solicit support, but of going out to create the enterprises and jobs for providing goods and services that become valuable assets to the building up of the neighborhoods themselves. These neighborhoods would support and market the products, which would in turn provide the support that these young urban missionaries themselves need.

Of course, we should partner with the rich, and with corporations, whenever possible. But we must not depend upon the rich to be benevolent enough. So we have to instill in our neighborhoods the mind-set and value system that sees our collective labor as mutually beneficial to all in local communities. Not only will this help build community; it will also help guard against false forms of dependency. Now just as we cannot depend upon the rich and corporations to be benevolent enough, we cannot let them go unchallenged when they practice greed; if we rely on them to meet our needs, we will be powerless to challenge their practices and will end up supporting their policies, which in effect oppress the poor. And just as we must be on guard against certain practices of the rich, those who lead these vital holistic urban ministry endeavors must make sure that the profits of their trade endeavors do not get poured into their own executives' salaries. A high percentage of the profits should go back into the communities (and not to the bank accounts and pocketbooks of executives, company boards, and stockholders who live outside the communities of greatest need) to further the quality of the services rendered and to nurture the people for whom such companies are responsible within these local communities.

I think the political system will help us to a certain degree, and I do not see anything wrong with receiving such help. But we must be ever mindful of the very real possibility that government may at times turn its back on us, even turning against us. So, solidarity at the grassroots level is essential in Christian community development.

We long for established churches, colleges, seminaries, businesses, and governmental agencies to join us in making these visions reality. But we cannot sit around, waiting for them to join us. If they do not join us, we will need to take ownership and lead the charge. We can take comfort from the fact that many great movements of God in the past did not emerge from within official structures. Instead they rose up as grassroots movements and spread like wildfire.

No doubt, this was what happened with the emergence of the Orders of the Catholic Church. The Orders did not originate with the popes or cardinals. The Orders emerged at the grassroots level as simple monks and other followers of Jesus burdened by the pressing problems of their day rose up and started tackling those problems. As a result of more and more people joining them, these grassroots movements became official Orders certified by the church. Mother Teresa was not sent out, but Sisters of Charity exists today because she and others went out. The Franciscan Order exists today because St. Francis of Assisi went out.

One way in which we can move forward is to go out into the neighborhoods in disrepair and start Bible clubs and house churches and let those grow and develop from a holistic perspective. Bible studies and house churches would serve as the spiritual bases of empowerment for community development work. The plan would include cultivating indigenous and local leaders from within these depressed neighborhoods and communities to take over leadership responsibilities. However we go about it though, we as God's people must become an incarnate presence, building healthy, revitalized communities today where reconciliation and redistribution occur. Such communities as these provide the greatest protection against consumerism and its negative impact on fringe minority groups and the poor.

We must begin seeing "quality of life" in terms of society and community, not in terms of the things we own and consume. We must come to see that true quality of life is people living together in love, joy, and peace. We must see that we can truly have quality of life only if we are cultivating good times with people from various sectors—eating together, playing together, fellowshipping together, not having to depend on going to the amusement park or movies for entertainment, for we the community are to be the amusement in our neighborhoods. Communities themselves must become this quality of life, beginning with Christ's people.

We must challenge our consumer culture, and *Consuming Jesus* does just that, even as it provides a theology of engagement on which to build. As we ask other people to get involved, we must take steps ourselves to become more authentic witnesses who demonstrate increasingly that we are in fact living by faith in God's Son, who loves us with an all-consuming love. Jesus says, "If anyone would come after me, let him deny himself and take up his cross daily and follow me." We have got to depend on the fact that Jesus said that if we seek first his kingdom and his righteousness, he will give us all that we truly need and rightly desire.

We can bank on our living Lord and Savior Jesus to follow through on what he has promised us. And so, we must aspire to live out the Lord's Prayer that his kingdom would come and his will would be done on earth *in our midst and in the midst of these needy communities* as it is in heaven.

As we follow the Lord Jesus, I firmly believe we are going to experience the love and joy of seeing the triune God at work in our lives and in our midst. Paul is fond of saying that we settle for so little when God calls us to so much more. We need to settle for more—much more of God's compassionate embrace of us so that we will extend that same compassion to the least of these in our world! I pray and hope that this book will serve as a source of inspiration that will spark a justice movement to spring forth from God's people's hearts and holistic lifestyles as Christ consumes us with his holy love in the power of the Spirit. God is at work within his children to will and to act according to his good pleasure. So, come join us as we join with God, and let's change the world!

JOHN M. PERKINS

Acknowledgments

This is a book about consumption and meals. At meals, it is the custom of many to give thanks to God and to those who have prepared the food, as well as to those who pass it their way. I give thanks to the triune God, who has spread before us a banqueting table where we consume Christ, who also consumes us and gives us the sustenance and strength to do battle with consumerism in the church and beyond. I also give thanks to those who have helped prepare and have passed the "food" to me. This book was written between meals in Princeton and Portland, and a host of places abroad and in between. I wish to express my sincere gratitude to the Center of Theological Inquiry in Princeton, New Jersey, for the privilege I had of serving as a resident member in 2004, during which time I began this book. Senior scholar-in-residence Robert Jenson, fellow resident members Peter Casarella, William Danaher, Paul Hanson, I-to Loh, Christo Lombard, Bruce McCormack, Evelyn Monsay, Gerbern Oegema, J. Jayakiran Sebastian, R. Kendall Soulen, William Storrar (C.T.I.'s current director), and Kenneth Williams, Wallace Alston (then director of C.T.I.), Kathi Morley and the staff of C.T.I., and my longtime friend Georg Pfleiderer, a visiting professor at Princeton Theological Seminary at the time — all provided invaluable insight, encouragement, critique, and support. I also wish to express thanks to my colleagues Al Baylis, Calvin Blom, Rick Calenberg, Barry Davis, Ron Frost, Marian O'Connor, and Roger Trautmann at Multnomah Bible College and Multnomah Biblical Seminary in Portland, Oregon, and special thanks

Acknowledgments

to Nathan Baxter, Brad Harper, and Jay Held for their significant engagement of the manuscript's development.

I am most grateful to Donald Brake, dean of the seminary, and Daniel Lockwood, Multnomah's president, who have supported the development of The Institute for the Theology of Culture: New Wine, New Wineskins, which I founded and direct. Several of New Wine's conferences and forums have allowed me the opportunity to reflect deeply and practically on the subject at hand. The following individuals deserve special merit: keynote speakers Ray Bakke, Tony Campolo, Ron Marlette, John M. Perkins, Richard Twiss, and Randy White; participants Joshua Butler, Kyogen Carlson, Zach Dundas, Donald Frazier, Rex Green, LeRoy Haynes, Jr., Peter Illyn, Tony Kriz, Letha McCleod, Donald Miller, Mikel Neumann, Elizabeth Perkins, Susan Slonaker, Emmett Wheatfall, and Richard White; and New Wine's Advisory Council — Derek Chinn, Ronn Elzinga, Phil Hobizal, Marcia Lyons, Seda Mansour, Steve Mitchell, David Sanford, and Michael Tso — along with Kindra Hakala, Sarah Speed, and Tracy Spitler. My students at Multnomah, especially my research assistant, Matthew Farlow, along with Wink Chin, Halden Doerge, Ross Halbach, Andreas Lunden, John Mayner, Elizabeth Myers, the "New Wine Makers," and those in my "Race, Class and Consumerism" and "Theology of Cultural Engagement" courses deserve mention for their important contribution to this book's development.

I also wish to express sincere appreciation to my parents, William and Audrey Metzger, and to Clarence Belnavis, J. Kameron Carter, Peter Cha, and Jane VanderPloeg; John Wenrich as well as the people of First Covenant Church in Portland, including Furlton Burns, Leonard and Esther Hallock, and Betty Ward; Clark Blakeman, Rick McKinley, Adam Rust, and Imago Dei Community in Portland; Barbara Feil, Ron Kincaid, Lindsey Smith, and Sunset Presbyterian Church in Beaverton, Oregon; John Shafe as well as Scott Frazier, Carl Palmer, and Bob Wall of Cedar Mill Bible Church in Portland; David and Henry Greenidge and Irvington Covenant Community Development Corporation; Tim Rogers, Harley and Emily Hayden, and the New Life Covenant Church in Atlanta; Sam and Sharon Mall and also Chicago International Evangelical Free Church; Timothy Peterson and the "Community Gathering" at Messiah College's Philadelphia campus; Steve Bilynskyj, Jon Stock, and participants of the 2005 Church and Culture Conference in Eugene, Oregon; Krisann Jarvis Foss and those in my workshop at the 2006 Crossing Borders Conference in Olympia, Washington; Brian Swarts and The Oregon Center for Christian Values, organizers of the Faith & American Values Summit 2006 at which I spoke; Dean Yuan and the attendees of the 2006 Home of Christ Retreat in Napa Valley, California, for numerous provisions and vintage inspiration and interaction regarding the subject at hand; Gary Ferngren and the Socratic Club at Oregon State University for hosting my two debates there; Steve Woodworth and Montreat College in North Carolina for their hospitality during my Spring 2007 Crossroads lectureship; Doug Flaherty, InterVarsity Christian Fellowship, the Student Diversity Alliance, and Multicultural Student Programs, University of North Carolina, Asheville, for their sponsorship of my "Religion & Culture" lectures, Spring 2007; and Zach Kincaid and those gathered for my talk at the Borders in Gresham, Oregon, which was part of the "Erasing Hate" national tour.

My wife, Mariko, has lived the making of this book with me through countless table conversations, reflections on the manuscript, and the joys and sorrows of our shared experience. She and our children, Christopher and Julianne, have sustained me with their laughter and their long-suffering love. I am most indebted to them. Many thanks go to Nancy Haught of *The Oregonian* for her feature essay on my work, as well as to Jon Pott, Linda Bieze, my editors Reinder Van Til and Jennifer Hoffman for their skill and expertise, David Bratt, and many others at Eerdmans for all their help in seeing this project to completion.

Index of Subjects and Names

Index of Scripture References